Taguchi Methods and QFD:

Hows and Whys for Management

Taguchi Methods and QFD:

Hows and Whys for Management

A special collection of papers and essays on today's
quality issues and new quality technologies

Nancy E. Ryan
Editor

ASI Press
Dearborn, Michigan

Published by the ASI Press, a division of the American Supplier Institute, Inc. Printed in the United States of America.

ISBN: 0-941243-04-4

Library of Congress Cataloging-in-Publication Data

Taguchi methods and QFD : hows and whys for management : a
    special collection of papers and essays on today's quality issues
    and new quality technologies / Nancy E. Ryan, editor.
        p.   cm.
    Papers presented at the Fifth Annual Symposium on Taguchi
Methods, conducted by the American Supplier Institute, October
8–9, 1987, in Detroit, Mich.
    ISBN 0-941243-04-4
    1. Quality control—Statistical methods—Congresses.
2. Production management—Quality control—Congresses.   I.
Ryan, Nancy E., 1959–   .   II. Symposium on Taguchi Methods (5th : 1987 : Detroit, Mich.)   III. American Supplier Institute.
TS156.T344 1988
658.5'62—dc19   88-22182
                                                              CIP

Contents

Preface

The papers and essays collected in this book reflect the insights and technical proficiency of senior industrial quality- and cost-improvement professionals with expertise in Taguchi Methods, Quality Function Deployment (QFD), and Company-Wide Quality Control (CWQC). In their respective papers and essays, these professionals discuss the need for and implementation of Taguchi Methods, QFD, and CWQC, as well as recount current successful applications in the automotive and other industrial environments.

The papers are primarily special presentations made at the Fifth Annual Taguchi Symposium, conducted by the American Supplier Institute (ASI), Inc., October 8–9, 1987, in Detroit, and at a unique seminar, "World-Class Competitive Leadership: Strategies for Senior Executives," sponsored by The University of Michigan's Office for the Study of Automotive Transportation (OSAT) and ASI, held November 18, 1987, in Dearborn, Michigan.

In addition, two of the papers were excerpted from two new titles from the ASI Press, *Quality by Design: Taguchi Methods and U.S. Industry* and *The Customer-Driven Company: Managerial Perspectives on QFD*. The former examines Dr. Genichi Taguchi's methodology and philosophy

from both a historical and a technical perspective, as well
as its increasing influence in the United States. The latter, an introduction to QFD and its related benefits, includes the insights and experiences of senior managers
from American companies that have applied the methodology.

ASI is a nonprofit organization dedicated to the ad-
vancement of quality management and the development
of new quality technologies that will enhance the competitive position of American industry. OSAT serves as
a focal point for a wide variety of research and communi-
cations activities related to automotive transportation,
and conducts an annual management-briefing seminar
attended by senior automotive-industry executives.
Both organizations are driving forces behind the current
evolution of American manufacturing and quality/pro-
ductivity practices.

Interest in Taguchi Methods, QFD, and CWQC is
snowballing as American companies that have imple-
mented them share their experiences and success stories
through case studies and public presentations. There is
already ample documentation showing how the application of these methodologies has enabled American companies to improve product quality and reduce costs and
product-development times, while gaining market share
in an increasingly competitive global marketplace.

John P. Kennedy
Director of Publishing
ASI Press
June 1988

Acknowledgments

The ASI Press is proud to have the opportunity to present these special papers and essays, and wishes to express its heartfelt appreciation to the following contributors for permitting publication of their papers:

Diane M. Byrne, ASI staff member (formerly Taguchi Methods Specialist, Eaton Corp.)

Dr. Don Clausing, Bernard M. Gordon Adjunct Professor of Manufacturing Innovation and Practice, Massachusetts Institute of Technology, Cambridge, Massachusetts

Dr. David Cole, Director, Office for the Study of Automotive Transportation, University of Michigan, Ann Arbor, Michigan, who also served as moderator of the "World-Class Competitive Leadership" seminar

Lance A. Ealey, automotive writer, Edison, New Jersey (formerly Principal Editor, *Automotive Industries*).

William E. Eureka, Vice President and General Manager, American Supplier Institute, Inc.

Robert H. Schaefer, Reliability Engineering Director, Product Assurance and Validation, Chevrolet-Pontiac-Canada Group, General Motors Corp., Warren, Michigan

ix

W. E. Scollard, Vice President of Manufacturing Operatons, Ford Motor Co., Dearborn, Michigan

Lawrence P. Sullivan, Chairman of the Board and Chief Executive Officer, American Supplier Institute, Inc., Dearborn, Michigan

David P. Williams, President and Chief Operating Officer, The Budd Co., Troy, Michigan

.1.

World-Class Quality, World-Class Cost

Dr. David Cole

I was recently in Phoenix, Arizona, for a meeting of a group called the International Automotive Forum and spoke with representatives from Japanese, American, and European industry. One of the clear messages from discussions with key industry leaders from around the world is that everybody is very cautious, fearful, and under extreme pressure in today's competitive environment. To ensure success and perhaps even long-range survival in this challenging world, we must develop the best possible skills and techniques related to the entire quality and cost issue.

I'd like to make a few statements regarding events in today's automotive industry. One of the most important facts is that we are in an extremely dynamic period. A few years ago, we recognized that change was going to be an important part of the automotive industry's future. Most, I think, envisioned this change as a shift from one plateau to another, and thought that once we

Dr. David Cole is Director of the Office for the Study of Automotive Transportation, University of Michigan, Ann Arbor, Michigan.

1

attained this new level, we'd get back to some semblance of business as usual. However, a more contemporary view is that there will not be stability or leveling off of change in the future, and, in fact, the future will probably bring us continuous change.

Another changing perception involves the breadth of the competition. It's no longer one North American manufacturer versus another domestic manufacturer; rather, we're in an all-inclusive competitive environment that consists of each of the world's automotive manufacturers, as well as their suppliers. The competition runs far deeper than we've witnessed in the past and is clearly the major driving force reshaping the industry.

Another basic factor we must consider is the level of overcapacity that's developing in the United States, which is somewhat similar to the overcapacity that already exists in Europe and Japan. There's no question that with this emerging overcapacity we will increasingly be in a customer-driven market rather than a manufacturer-defined market.

One of the most important factors in this growing global competition is the role that North American-transplant manufacturers and suppliers will play in the future. The transplant production volume forecast for 1995 is nearly three million units. Clearly, these transplant manufacturers—or more appropriately, new North American manufacturers—have major expectations for building and selling cars here.

The gravity of this competitive challenge is illustrated by some of the inherent advantages these transplant manufacturers possess. Simply put, they're coming to the party with new production systems and management systems, as well as a very carefully selected and highly trained work force to match these systems. This new and youthful work force has none of the benefit costs associated with older and retired workers. At Honda's Marysville, Ohio, plant, for example, the average worker age is 28. The transplant manufacturers also enjoy some favorable exchange-rate considerations: The Japanese generated substantial earnings here in the early 1980s, when the yen/dollar ratio was about 250:1. The dollars were converted to yens and returned to Japan. With the Japanese currency now much stronger, the original profits buy more dollars of investment than they would have several years ago. Additionally, significant economic-development support has been made available to the various transplants.

These are formidable competitive advantages that must be overcome if our traditional automotive manufacturers and suppliers are going to survive in the years ahead.

We might argue about who is number one in the world in automotive manufacturing. But the consensus at the manufacturer's level is that Toyota Motor Corp. is probably number one in terms of production system, management system, and low cost. It's also important to understand that Toyota and its peers are hardly standing still. It's evident from talking to Toyota executives that they are moving very aggressively forward to reduce costs, improve productivity, and introduce new products because of the pressures of the international marketplace, especially the accelerating value of the yen compared to the dollar. We must understand that the competition represents a moving target, and that to be a winner in the years ahead, we must not just aim *at* the

Toyotas of the world, we must aim far *ahead* of where they are today.

One of the clear lessons of the last few years relates to the proper role of management and technology in a modern automotive plant. This was clearly demonstrated in the Toyota/General Motors Corp. joint venture, NUMMI (New United Motors Manufacturing, Inc.), in Fremont, California, which showed the importance of an effective management system in improving quality and productivity. What can be concluded from this experiment—and many other experiments where we've observed these new management systems applied to the American work force—is that step one isn't investing in new technology or investing for investment's sake. Rather, step one is learning how to manage our existing production system properly, which then creates a foundation for the application of advanced technology.

Another important point demonstrated by operations like NUMMI is the importance of "systems" thinking—the proper interrelationship of all factors that are part of the planning, design, production, selling, and servicing of vehicles and parts. In our culture, we tend to think in terms of narrow disciplines without appropriate linkages of the various elements of the production system. In a systems organization like NUMMI, there's tremendous attention to detail, but it's always integrated into the total system. Systems mentality is a very important success factor for the future.

Yet another issue relates to today's global environment. We have a tendency to look at a competitor's product and say, "That's our competition," whereas in fact that's the product of the competitor's thinking *four or five years before.* We need to understand our competitors, their culture, language, and, in general, how they think. We need to better understand the *people* we are competing against in a global environment, not just their products.

We are going through a fundamental period of industry restructuring in North America. Every facet of the automotive industry is in transition—management systems, production systems, labor-management relationships, manufacturer-supplier relationships, design and manufacturing processes, and the selling and service system are undergoing a fundamental change. In light of this, let's trace step by step the restructuring of the automotive industry.

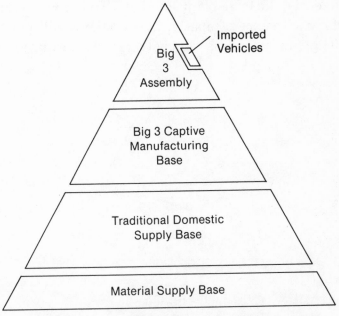

Figure 1–1. As shown here and in Figures 1–2 to 1–5, the domestic automotive industry has undergone an incremental restructuring. The configuration of today's industry (Figure 1–5) is much different from the above rather simple configuration of the past.

The automotive industry used to have a rather simple configuration, as illustrated in **Figure 1-1**. It consisted of the major domestic manufacturers at the top of the pyramid, with a small role for imports. In the next layer is the large, allied supplier base, followed by a layer of outside component suppliers, and finally the material suppliers. As the restructuring has proceeded in incremental steps (see **Figures 1-1** to **1-5**), we've seen increased import penetration, movement of traditional component suppliers to a higher level of the supply structure, and excess capacity at all levels. The introduction of the transplant manufacturers followed and, subsequently, the transplant suppliers. Today, we see an industry with excess capacity at every level and a general shifting of suppliers downstream. For example, the

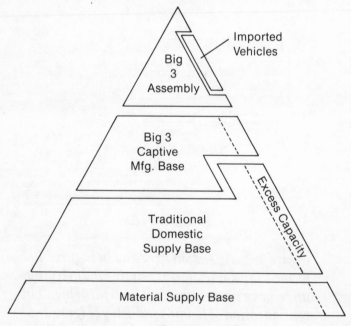

Figure 1-2.

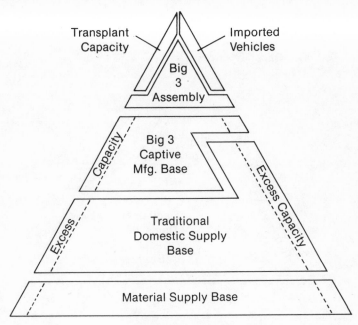

Figure 1–3.

material supplier is asking, "Where can I find added profit opportunities?" Of course, the answer is obvious—in the next level of the supply structure. Every level and every company in every level of the structure is experiencing the challenges of fundamental change.

The future market promises to be very tough and extremely exciting. There's no question that we are looking at a market where the customer will be "king" or "queen." It's going to be fast-changing and very competitive—the customer will have a tremendous array of choices. The customer will be more demanding and far less loyal than the customer of the past. Several observations are in order concerning the customer and quality. One is that "quality" is, in reality, many different factors—quality is what the customer perceives it to be.

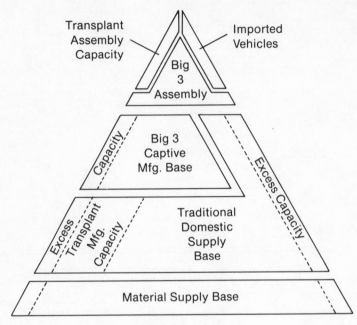

Figure 1-4.

Quality may not necessarily be what *we* define as quality; it's the *customer's* definition that counts in selling motor vehicles.

Secondly, it's clear that, prompted by competitive pressures, a general international equilibration of the various quality factors across all product lines is well under way. Beyond 1990, traditional quality factors will cease to differentiate products or markets. This is a fact of enormous significance to the industry as it prepares for the decade ahead.

In the future of the automotive industry, I do not believe that quality and cost will lead to competitive advantage. Rather, I think that world-class quality and world-class cost are just tickets to the playing field where the real competition will be fought—that unless

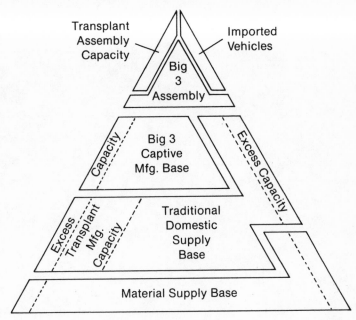

Figure 1–5.

you have world-class quality and world-class cost, you won't even have a chance to compete. And unless you effectively utilize the best skills and techniques available, you won't attain the world-class quality and cost levels necessary to remain in the game with a chance to win.

. 2 .

Taguchi Methods

Diane M. Byrne

"The quality of a product is the (minimum) loss imparted to the society from the time the product is shipped."

—Dr. Genichi Taguchi

Fundamental to Dr. Genichi Taguchi's approach to Quality Engineering is the concept of loss. When *we* think of loss to society, things that come to mind include air pollution, excessive noise from a car without a muffler, or a chemical leak from a nuclear power plant. Dr. Taguchi views loss to society on a much broader scale. He associates loss with every product that meets the consumer's hand. This loss includes, among other things, consumer dissatisfaction, added warranty costs to the producer, and loss due to a company's having a bad reputation, which leads to eventual loss of market share.

The idea of minimizing loss to society is rather abstract and thus difficult to deal with as a company objective. When we consider loss to society to be long-term

Diane M. Byrne, formerly a specialist in Taguchi Methods at the Eaton Corp., Southfield, Michigan, is now a staff member of the American Supplier Institute, Inc., Dearborn, Michigan.

11

loss to our company, however (and the two are equivalent), the definition may have more meaning.

We usually quantify (or attempt to quantify) our quality costs in terms of scrap and rework, warranty, or other tangible items. These, however, constitute only the tip of the iceberg. What about the hidden costs or long-term losses related to engineering/management time, inventory, customer dissatisfaction, and losing market share in the long run? Can we quantify these kinds of losses? Perhaps, but not accurately. Indeed, we need a way to approximate these hidden and long-term losses, because they're the largest contributors to total quality loss. Dr. Taguchi uses the Quality Loss Function (QLF) for this purpose.

The way in which the QLF is established depends on the type of quality characteristic involved. A quality characteristic is whatever we measure to judge performance (quality). There are five types of quality characteristics: nominal the best (achieving a desired target value with minimal variation—e.g., dimension and output voltage), smaller the better (minimizing a response— e.g., shrinkage and wear), larger the better (maximizing a response—e.g., pull-off force and tensile strength), attribute (classifying and/or counting data—e.g., appearance), and dynamic (response varies depending on input—e.g., speed of a fan drive should vary depending on the engine temperature).

The QLF will now be demonstrated for a nominal-the-best quality characteristic. From an engineering standpoint, the losses of concern are those caused when a product's quality characteristic deviates from its desired target value. For example, consider an AC-DC converting circuit where the AC input is 110 volts and the circuit is to output 115 DC volts, as typically used for a television set. The output voltage is the quality characteristic of interest, and its desired target value is 115 volts. Any deviation from 115 volts is considered functional variation and will cause some loss.

Suppose there are four factories producing these circuits under the same specifications, 115 +/- 3 volts, and their output is as shown in **Figure 2-1**. Suppose further that all four factories carry out 100% inspection (let's even naively assume it's 100% effective), so that only those pieces within specifications are shipped out. If you're the consumer and wish to buy the circuits from one of the four factories, which would you choose, assuming that the price is the same?

While all four factories are shipping out circuits that meet the engineering specifications, Factory No. 4 appears to offer a more uniform product; i.e., the variation around the 115-volt target is less at this factory than at the three other factories.

**Output Distribution
from Four Factories**

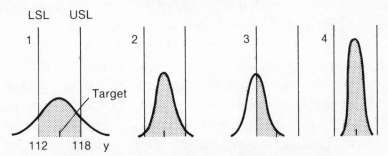

Figure 2-1. Each of these four factories is shipping products that meet engineering specifications. Factory No. 4, however, is producing a more uniform product.

In this way of thinking, loss occurs not only when a product is outside the specifications, but also when a product falls within the specifications. Further, it's reasonable to believe that loss continually increases as a product deviates further from the target value, as the parabola (QLF) in **Figure 2-2** illustrates. While a loss function may take on many forms, Dr. Taguchi has found that the simple quadratic function approximates the behavior of loss in many instances. For smaller-the-better quality characteristics, such as part shrinkage, or larger-the-better quality characteristics, such as tensile strength, the QLF may become a half parabola. In any event, belief in the QLF promotes efforts to continually reduce the variation in a product's quality characteristics. Dr. Taguchi's Quality Engineering methodology is a vehicle for attaining such improvements.

The QLF was used to estimate the average quality loss from each of the four factories, as illustrated in **Figure 2-3**. Notice that the smallest average quality loss was obtained from Factory No. 4, the factory with the highest quality. In short, the QLF is a measure of quality in monetary units that reflects not only immediate costs, such as scrap and rework, but long-term losses as well.

When optimizing a product or process, our goal is generally to reduce variability; when we reduce variability, we'd also like to reduce cost. Dr. Taguchi often says that an engineer's task isn't merely to develop a system that will work, since there are many alternatives for a system. Rather, the engineer's job is to find a system that will work *and* be cost-effective.

To minimize loss, we're faced with the task of producing a product at optimum levels and with minimal variation in its quality characteristics. Two types of factors

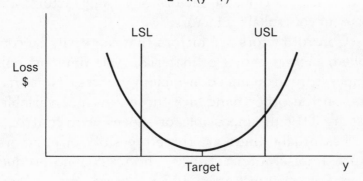

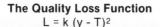

L = loss in $'s
k = cost coefficient
y = value of quality characteristic
T = target value

Figure 2-2. Dr. Taguchi has found that loss continually increases as a product deviates further from the target value. In many instances, a simple quadratic function approximates the behavior of loss.

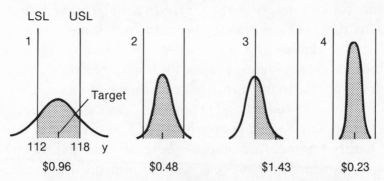

Figure 2-3. The smallest average quality loss was obtained from Factory No. 4, the factory with the highest quality.

affect a product's quality characteristics: control factors (also called controllable factors or design factors) and noise (uncontrollable) factors.

Control factors are factors that can easily be controlled, such as choice of material, cycle time, or mold temperature in an injection-molding process. Noise factors, on the other hand, are those nuisance variables that are difficult, impossible, or expensive to control.

Essentially, there are three types of noise factors: external noise, internal noise, and product-to-product noise. For an injection-molding process, the ambient temperature and humidity are external noises, the aging of the machinery and tolerances on the process factors are internal noises, and manufacturing imperfections are generally responsible for product-to-product noise.

Noise factors are usually responsible for causing a product's quality characteristics to deviate from their target values. Is our goal to identify the most guilty noise factors so we can attempt to control them? No! Remember, controlling noise factors is very costly, if not impossible. Instead, we'd prefer to select values for our control factors so that the product or process is least sensitive to changes in the noise factors. Instead of finding and eliminating the causes, which are often noise factors, we remove or reduce the impact of the causes. In doing so, we make our products robust against noise.

Robust product and process designs can be achieved through Dr. Taguchi's approach to Quality Engineering. Quality Engineering involves both off-line quality control (product and process design) and on-line quality control (process monitoring and control) activities.

Product quality must be engineered in! This is the thrust of Dr. Taguchi's off-line quality-control activities, which involve both product design and process design. The three steps that are involved in the engineering optimization of a product or process are: system design, parameter design, and tolerance design.

System design involves innovation and requires knowledge from the fields of science and engineering. It includes the selection of materials, parts, and tentative product-parameter values (during product design) and the selection of production equipment and tentative values for process factors (during process design).

The tentative nominal values are then tested over specified ranges during parameter design, and the best combination of levels is determined. Parameter design determines the product-parameter values and the operating levels of process factors that are least sensitive to change in environmental conditions and other noise factors. This is the key step for achieving high quality without an increase in cost.

Finally, tolerance design is employed if the reduced variation obtained through parameter design isn't sufficient. Tolerance design involves tightening tolerances on product parameters or process factors whose variations impart a large influence on the output variation. In other words, tolerance design typically means spending money—buying better-grade materials, components, or machinery.

In the United States, most engineers are conditioned to spend money to reach required product-performance levels. They jump from system design to tolerance design, omitting the step where they likely have the most to gain in terms of cost and quality—the step Japanese engineers do so well—parameter design.

Parameter design is the key stage of Dr. Taguchi's

methodology. This is where we have the most to gain in terms of improving quality without simultaneously increasing cost. The objective of parameter design is to find the nominal values for the controllable factors so that maximum product performance is achieved with minimal sensitivity to noise, and to do so at the lowest cost.

The strategy of parameter design is to recognize control factors and noise factors and to treat them separately. In the data analysis, a Signal-to-Noise Ratio (S/N Ratio) is used as a measure of performance. The S/N Ratio is inversely proportional to the QLF. To maximize the S/N Ratio is to minimize loss, which means improving quality.

Parameter design and the S/N Ratio will now be demonstrated for a nominal-the-best characteristic. The example involves the manufacture of a specific metal product that's currently in the research stage at the Eaton Corp.

Example

Metal disks, 0.256-in. target thickness, are being produced from a press in the Eaton research laboratory. Although several quality characteristics were identified as important, thickness was regarded as the most important. The objective of this experiment was to find the appropriate combination of press parameters that will minimize piece-to-piece variation in disk thickness while the product is still in the research stage.

Six press parameters (control factors) were identified that may affect thickness. These factors were set at two levels (low and high) during the experiment, as shown in **Figure 2–4**.

Press Parameters	
Control Factors	Levels
A. Press Parameter 1	Low High
B. Press Parameter 2	Low High
C. Press Parameter 3	Low High
D. Press Parameter 4	Low High
E. Press Parameter 5	Low High
F. Press Parameter 6	Low High

Figure 2–4. The six press parameters (control factors) that may affect disk thickness were set at two levels (low and high) during the experiment.

The level of raw material in the hopper will vary during manufacturing. Therefore, the raw-material level was identified as a noise factor to be optimized against.

Twenty disks were produced at each control-factor condition: 10 disks when the raw material was low and 10 disks when the raw material was high. A S/N Ratio was computed for each test condition of the control factors (see **Figure 2–5**). The S/N Ratio used in this case considered only variation. A high S/N Ratio means that less variation is present.

First, an analysis of the S/N Ratios was performed. Through this analysis, factors that affect variation were identified. **Figure 2–6** illustrates the effect of Factor A, Press Parameter 1. The highest S/N Ratio was found when Factor A was at its high level. Thus, the high level of Factor A was selected, because it gives the best performance (the least variation).

A similar analysis was done for Factors B through F. It was found that four of the six factors affect variation: Factors A, C, E, and F.

A second analysis was then performed on the raw

S/N Ratios for Control Factors

	A B C D E F	Low Material		High Material		S/N
1	1 1 1 1 1 1	0.2598	0.2596	0.2548	0.2554	39.9
		0.2598	0.2600	0.2555	0.2555	
		0.2593	0.2582	0.2548	0.2551	
		0.2600	0.2608	0.2544	0.2549	
		0.2606	0.2602	0.2545	0.2541	
2	1 1 2 2 2 2	0.2552	0.2562	0.2525	0.2534	44.4
		0.2566	0.2565	0.2537	0.2532	
3	1 2 1 1 2 2					39.6
4	1 2 2 2 1 1					44.2
5	2 1 1 2 1 2					42.5
6	2 1 2 1 2 1					53.1
7	2 2 1 2 2 1					50.4
8	2 2 2 1 1 2					43.9

Figure 2–5. A Signal-to-Noise Ratio was computed for each test condition of the control factors. A high ratio means that less variation is present.

data. Through this analysis, the factors that affect the mean were identified. It was found that five of the six control factors affect the mean: Factors A, B, C, E, and F. Four of these factors (A, C, E, and F) also affected variation. Since Factors A, C, E, and F affect variation, they will be controlled to minimize variation. Factor B affects the mean but not variation. Thus, Factor B is used as a signal factor to shift the mean to the target.

In the final combination of factors, Factors A (high level), C (high level) and F (low level) were controlled to minimize variation, B (low level) was adjusted to shift the mean to the target, and D (low level) and E (low level) were controlled to increase productivity.

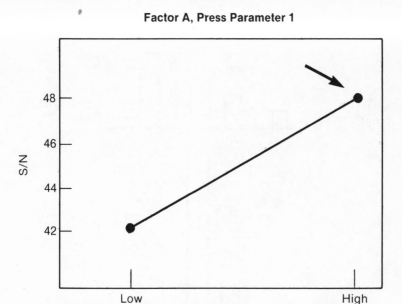

Figure 2–6. The highest Signal-to-Noise Ratio was found when Factor A was at its high level. The high level was thus selected, because it gives the least variation.

Before the experiment was conducted, the technician finely adjusted the press. The best standard deviation he could achieve was s = 0.00106. Operating at the combination of press parameters determined through the study, standard deviation was reduced to s = 0.00029 (see **Figure 2–7**). If the experiment hadn't been conducted, the manufacturing capability of this metal product would have been dramatically underestimated.

In summary, the Taguchi approach to Quality Engineering encompasses all stages of product development. The key step for achieving high quality and low

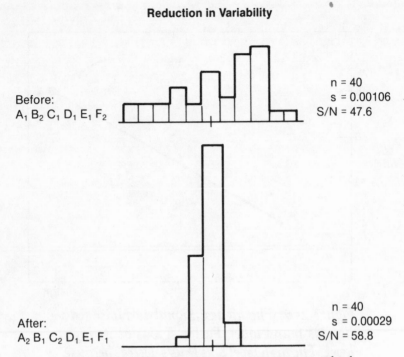

Figure 2–7. The experiment at Eaton resulted in a dramatic reduction in variability. With the new combination of press parameters, standard deviation was reduced from 0.00106 to 0.00029.

cost, however, is the stage called parameter design. Through parameter design, levels of product and process factors are determined so that the product's quality characteristics are optimized and the effects of noise factors are minimized. The S/N Ratio is used as a measure of performance in the data analysis. To maximize the S/N Ratio is to minimize loss, thus improving quality.

. 3 .

Design Engineering

Lance A. Ealey

There's a legendary comment concerning Rolls-Royce that was made during the long reign of the incredibly durable and beautiful automobile that became known as the Silver Ghost, the car that first earned Rolls-Royce its "best car in the world" tag line. The remark was made by a competing luxury-car builder, and it wasn't meant as a compliment. The Rolls-Royce, he said, is a triumph of craftsmanship over design . . . .

The first Rolls-Royce was designed and built by English engineer Sir Frederick Henry Royce. Royce's approach to car building was to "engineer" his designs to perfection, no matter what the cost. That's not to take anything away from Rolls-Royce: For the few who could afford them, Silver Ghosts were, indeed, the best cars in the world. Unfortunately, buying a Rolls-Royce just wasn't an option for most duffers of that time (or even our own).

If you substitute the word "engineering" for "craftsmanship," the disgruntled competitor's comment con-

This chapter is excerpted from *Quality by Design: Taguchi Methods and U.S. Industry*, published by the ASI Press. Lance A. Ealey is the former principal editor of *Automotive Industries*.

23

cerning Rolls-Royce points to one of the major differences in the way Japanese and Western automakers approach the task of designing and building cars.

Designs on Sale

Contrary to popular belief, manufacturers today *aren't selling products; they're selling product designs.* When you get right down to it, the real trench warfare in the marketplace is being waged in design studios, not on assembly lines or in retail markets. A good design works for the company—it's easy to build, it's cost-effective, and it performs in the marketplace. A bad design, on the other hand, is your competition's best friend—stealing downstream-engineering cost and effort, ensuring a high number of product start-up problems, and generally making life both costly and miserable for everyone from engineering to manufacturing to sales. Product design impacts every downstream operation in a company. If a company's designs aren't up to snuff—if they're not robust, if they're still green—there's little you can do to compensate for it. The company won't be able to offer the product at a competitive price and still be assured that the product will perform in the marketplace with a minimum of warranty costs or loss of goodwill. Your competitors from Japan, on the other hand, are taking great pains to optimize their designs.

What Taguchi Offers

For an example of the power of parameter design, let's look at an imaginary product-design cycle for competing U.S. and Japanese television companies. Both companies develop new TV sets. Through exhaustive system-design work, each set has been designed with many unique features, including voice-activated channel selection. Through close examination, however, an informed observer would recognize that the American design at this point clearly holds the advantage in terms of innovation.

After system design is complete, the Americans set about engineering the various circuits so that they conform to the given specifications. In order to maintain a high-quality picture, the American engineers set certain critical tolerances very tightly. To achieve these tolerances, high-quality components are specified, and these significantly raise the consumer price for the TV.

The Japanese, after coming up with a system design, go through the parameter-design stage. During this stage, they optimize the performance of various aspects of the TV using the cheapest possible components. Because they've optimized the various circuits during parameter design, the need to specify very tight tolerances during the tolerance-design stage is greatly reduced. The Japanese utilize Taguchi's experimental-design techniques during both parameter and tolerance design to quickly and cost-effectively determine design and tolerance levels for the TV. They also discover that they can replace certain design elements with cheaper components without affecting picture quality or set reliability.

Both TVs are introduced to the market. The Japanese TV comes to market some three months earlier than the American TV, and quickly gains a reputation as a high-quality/high-value unit. The American TV is late because various circuits had to be redesigned that were adversely affected by various ambient-temperature and humidity levels discovered during last-minute prototype testing. Cost overruns in several areas, including unanticipated production problems occurring with the voice-activated channel selector, have forced the Ameri-

can manufacturer to drop several of the innovative sales
points from his TV—including the channel selector. The
TV is quickly redesigned to feature a conventional
channel tuner. The American manager is shocked to see
that the Japanese TV—with voice-activated channel
selector—is selling for less than the projected price of his
TV. He orders his engineers to reduce the cost of the TV
by respec'ing certain noncritical circuits using cheaper
components. After six months on the market, the American manufacturer is inundated with customer com-
plaints and warranty costs, because the TV's performance and reliability, when compared with its Japanese
competition, aren't even in the same ballpark. Many of
these warranty costs, incidentally, can be traced back to
the cheaper components that were substituted at the
last minute for more costly, higher-quality parts.

   Many industries, including the bulk of the televi-
sion-building industry, have moved out of the United
States. The reason typically given for moving offshore is
that the company can't compete because of the cost of
the U.S. labor force. When the Japanese yen gained in
value by more than 50% in the mid-1980s, everyone in
the United States expected the American trade deficit
with Japan to shrink considerably. In many cases, U.S.
products had become as inexpensive as Japan's, the rea-
soning went, so Americans should start buying U.S.-
made alternatives. Instead, the U.S. trade deficit with
Japan actually continued to grow for some time. Why?
The Japanese have proven that consumers are willing to
buy a quality product even if they must pay a premium
price for it. Reducing labor costs is only a small part of
the competitive equation. It's the easy part, too; that's
why so many companies have hurried offshore with

their products. But if low labor costs are the only thing an offshore venture is bringing to the party, its long-term competitive ability in a sophisticated market such as the United States will be a very "iffy" thing.

The more difficult, although ultimately more lucrative, route to becoming competitive starts with design.

Using It Because It Works

Dr. Genichi Taguchi's Quality Engineering techniques put maximum analytical power in the hands of design engineers. In fact, Taguchi Methods were custom-designed for engineers by a brilliant engineer, and an important ingredient of their success is the special knowledge an engineer has of a product or process. This knowledge is what makes it possible to shortcut traditional test-every-combination experiments.

In a very real sense, your successes with Taguchi Methods will be tied directly to the savvy of your engineers. Taguchi Methods allow an engineer to organize his thinking and to deal exclusively with facts. They provide a road map that leads an engineer to the optimum levels of performance a product or process can achieve without adding cost.

Traditionally, as noted above, finding the optimum level of performance for a product or process has been something of a crapshoot in American industry. A product would be designed to meet certain artificially set performance criteria. Specification limits for a product are usually set according to inherited knowledge of that product—in other words, if it worked on the last version, it'll work on this one, too. Your engineers would eventually get you close to your target, often by spec'ing

closer-than-necessary tolerances and higher-perfor-
mance/higher-cost critical components. Many times,
that higher-cost component could have been replaced by
a lower-cost device that had been optimized to its fullest.

The analogy of looking for a needle in a haystack is a
good one in describing traditional product- and process-
design techniques. There can be literally thousands of
ways that a complex product can be put together. Testing every combination of variables is impossible in a
manufacturing environment, because problems tend to
be fairly complex and time is almost always in short
supply. Some combinations will give you optimum results, but not for the minimum cost. Traditionally,
unless an engineer performs a full-blown design of
experiments, testing every combination of factors and
interactions through an almost endless series of experiments, he has no way of knowing if the combination of
design factors he chose while designing a product was
the best possible combination.

Taguchi's methodology allows the design engineer
to shortcut that long, drawn-out procedure, and it allows him to do it without the aid of a trained statistician.

Training

An engineer can usually grasp enough of the fun-
damentals of Taguchi's off-line quality-control techniques to begin performing process-related design experiments after a week's training in Taguchi Methods.
Be aware, however, that it takes years for an engineer to
become an expert.

Within many Japanese companies, training in Taguchi Methods is considered a necessary and continuing

part of every engineer's education. A Japanese engineer without knowledge of Taguchi Methods is said to be only half an engineer. Most of this training is done in-house, and is augmented by regularly scheduled symposia during which particularly interesting and successful case studies are presented. (It's been Taguchi's philosophy that the only way to truly understand his methodology is by participating in Quality Engineering case studies.)

Within the United States, Ford is a recognized leader in promoting Taguchi Methods training—not only for its own engineers, but for those of supplier companies as well. The ITT Automotive Group also has an aggressive in-house Taguchi Methods training program. AT&T Bell Laboratories is also a leader in in-house training, as is Xerox Corp. Still, compared with leading Japanese companies, the Americans are just beginning to climb the steepest part of the Taguchi Methods learning curve. It has been estimated that many Japanese engineers complete as many as 600 hours of training in Taguchi Methods.

Nippondenso Co., Ltd., for example, despite having more than 30 years of experience in Taguchi Methods, retains a very aggressive Taguchi Methods training schedule. About 15% of Nippondenso's 6,000-person engineering staff is considered expert in the methods, and another 30% is very competent.

The rest of the engineering staff is taught and advised by 918 expert practitioners. By comparison, only a relative handful of the engineers in most leading American companies that have embraced Taguchi Methods have even gone through preliminary Taguchi Methods training. And the number of experts in Taguchi Methods in the entire United States can literally be counted on one's fingers.

At Nippondenso, all new engineering employees go through a four-day introductory course in experimental design. Nippondenso trains about 400 people per year in this course. Within three to seven years of employment, engineers are given an additional 12-day course in the use of various Taguchi Methods techniques, including orthogonal arrays and the QLF.

Within five to nine years of employment, engineers go through an advanced 11-day session of Taguchi Methods. Additionally, reliability engineers take a separate course in parameter design and tolerance design, and engineering assistant managers attend a seven-day session on the entire system.[1]

An important part of the training is to have all trainees produce case studies for critique. Nippondenso, however, is something of a special case; it's one of the premier users of Taguchi Methods in Japan, and its training program reflects this fact.

A more typical example of experimental-design training comes from the Sharp Corp., which introduced Taguchi Methods ten years ago. Sharp provides roughly nine days of Taguchi Methods training a year for its engineering staff. It also requires engineers to attend yearly design-of-experiments seminars, which are sponsored by the Japanese Standards Association and taught by Taguchi himself. Taguchi is often retained to teach his methodology at Japanese companies. Apart from

---

1. "The History of Nippondenso Activities of Application of the Taguchi Method," April 1987. Provided by Nippondenso Co. Ltd.

formal training sessions, the bulk of real understanding concerning Taguchi Methods comes as engineers use the techniques in the course of their daily work, aided by more experienced practitioners.[2]

Theory, Computer Simulation, and Taguchi Methods

The traditional approach when undertaking a Taguchi Methods design of experiments is to lay out the experiments using an orthogonal array,* perform each experiment, and then record and analyze your data. However, the advent of accessible computers allows an experimenter to perform certain parameter- and tolerance-design case studies on a theoretical level. In situations where scientific theory exists for the actions and reactions of factors, it's possible to "perform" orthogonal-array experiments totally within the circuits of a computer. Taguchi has long advocated the use of theory in his experimental-design philosophy, since it's often more cost-effective to perform experiments on paper or in a computer than it is to physically conduct experiments.

Engineers at General Motors Corp.'s Detroit Diesel Allison Division performed just such an experimental design in developing a theoretical diesel-engine design. While the program was given a proposed budget of

---

2. Information supplied by Sharp Corp., Osaka, Japan, April 1987.

*An orthogonal array is a matrix of numbers arranged in rows and columns, each row representing the state of the factors and each column representing a specific factor that can be changed from experiment to experiment.

$10,000, the entire system was run on computer for less than $400.[3]

The engineers wanted to develop a theoretical engine of the future that would identify which combination of engine-design features would generate optimum levels of fuel efficiency.

The engineers used a computer simulation program that acted in effect as their "engine." Six factors were to be evaluated, and in each case the "engine's" goal was to generate 300 horsepower at an engine speed of 1,800 revolutions per minute. The engineers also suspected that there were three interactions between three factors that could have significant effects on the performance outcome of the engine.

The engineers assigned the six main factors to a 27-experiment (L_{27}) orthogonal array and ran the experiments on their computer-simulated "engine." Each factor was to be tested at three different operating levels. A little quick math will show that to perform a full factorial experimental design, during which every possible combination of the six factors at three levels is tested, GM would have had to run 729 experiments. The engineers came to the conclusion that even using a high-speed computer, a computer simulation of a full-factorial design of experiments would take too long to accomplish.

And if GM had elected to perform 27 experiments involving structural changes to the engine, the company would have had to construct the equivalent of 27 different engine configurations. While engineers will usually use one-cylinder test engines that can be reconfigured to

---

3. Jerry Roslund and Mustafa Savliwala, "A Theoretical Engine Design Using a Taguchi Factorial," presented at University of Michigan Quality Assurance Seminar, Aug. 1986, Traverse City, Michigan.

replicate the 27 combinations of factors, the time and money spent to do so would be many times as expensive as the computer simulation.

After running the experiments, the GM engineers analyzed the data using a commercial personal-computer software program. This program is custom-tailored for Taguchi Methods experimental-design analysis, and it does most of the tedious and exacting number crunching, thus reducing the chances of calculation error.

The optimum levels of the six factors were revealed during analysis, and a confirmation run using these factor levels proved the superior fuel efficiency of this "engine." Best of all, the engineers calculated that the simulator-driven Taguchi Methods experimental design generated a 17-to-1 return on investment based on the cost of the project and the man-months needed to complete it.

Intelligent Orthogonal Arrays

Today, it's possible to perform parameter-design experiments via computer simulation, removing much cost and drudgery from the experimental-design process. But what about tomorrow?

Just as computers themselves have become more user-friendly over the years, recent development work at Bell Labs indicates that the full power of Taguchi's experimental-design system could soon become even more accessible to engineers.

Madhav Phadke and two colleagues, Newton Lee and Rajiv Keny, have developed an expert system for experimental-design techniques that automates the selection of an orthogonal array and the design of an experiment. The Prolog-based computer-software system uses artificial intelligence to assist less-than-expert practitioners in the design of complex experimentation.[4]

The prototype system, which was developed to assist AT&T engineers in running Taguchi Methods experiments, asks the experimenter a few questions concerning the experiment to be planned and then suggests an appropriate orthogonal-array design that could be used for the experiment.

There are 17 basic orthogonal arrays that engineers generally choose from. These 17 arrays run from the L_4, which will accommodate three two-level factors arranged in four different experiments, to the L_{81}, which will accommodate 40 three-level factors arranged in 81 different experiments.

While in many basic experiments the selection of an orthogonal array can be fairly clear-cut, some applications can be quite complicated. For example, in several arrays that can accommodate only two-level factors, it's possible to combine two columns of two-level factors, thereby creating the equivalent of a four-level factors column. There are also certain arrays that are best suited for dealing with the main effects of control factors.

Bell Labs' expert system will also assign the factors to specific columns in the orthogonal array using a computerized version of Taguchi's linear graphs. A linear graph is a one-dimensional depiction of the relationships between columns in the orthogonal array. Every column

---

4. Telephone interview with Madhav S. Phadke, Aug. 1987. Also, Newton S. Lee et al, "An Expert System for Experimental Design: Automating the Design of Orthogonal Array Experiments," *ASQC Quality Congress Transactions*, 1987.

in the orthogonal array is represented by either a dot or a line drawn between two dots. The columns represented by lines indicate that those columns may be used to observe the interactions between the two dots (columns) they join. While a limited number of linear graphs are usually used for each array, an experimenter facing unique requirements may wish to tap more unusual linear-graph arrangements. The number of graphs available for certain arrays can be formidable.

The expert system is able to handle complex or simple linear graphs equally well, and commits no mental errors or silly mistakes. As it stands now, Bell Labs' software can solve roughly 85% of the real-world experimental-design problems it would face in the field.

Future goals include teaching the system "tricks," such as combining noninteractive factors on a single orthogonal-array column so that a smaller array could be used, which would reduce the number (and cost) of experiments.

Another area under study involves problem solving. For example, the system could suggest to the user that by dropping noncritical factors, the experiment could run on a smaller orthogonal array—again, with cost cutting in mind.

In addition to other refinements, the software designers are exploring the possibility of giving the system an explanation capability. This would allow the software to explain why it made certain decisions and recommendations in the layout of the experiment, thereby functioning as a teaching element. At present, AT&T has no plans to sell the system outside of the company, but such research points to the day when any moderately trained practitioner will be able to tap into expertise concerning Taguchi Methods any time a need arises.

· 4 ·

Taguchi: A Managerial Perspective

David P. Williams

Doing business in today's marketplace is challenging, but it's also very exciting. We know that success today and in the future requires recognition, understanding, and utilization of every improvement strategy that fits our individual needs.

The pursuit of world-class quality seems to require movement through several phases. Phase one might be recognizing the need for change. Phases two through three, four, and maybe even five could be thought of as progressing through management commitment, involvement, communication, and all those things that deal with the desire to seek continuous quality improvement. The desire for world-class quality and the reaching of that destination are miles apart. Now we're looking for the tools that will pave the road.

One such tool is Dr. Genichi Taguchi's Quality Engineering methodology. Taguchi Methods reduce costs through reduction of variation, which will always result in improved quality, and allow designs and processes to

David P. Williams is President and Chief Operating Officer of The Budd Co., Troy, Michigan.

be optimized in a way that makes them insensitive to factors beyond the manufacturer's control. Now that's about as technical as I get. All I know is that it has helped us improve quality and, at the same time, reduce costs associated with scrap, inspection, and rework. Moreover, it has delivered quick results with little investment.

This past summer, The Budd Co. launched its third company-wide Taguchi Methods Design of Experiments seminar. About 40 engineers attended five days of off-site classroom training. At that time, we completed training approximately 120 people from our divisions and plants. The two previous seminars, held in October 1986 and March 1987, resulted in more than 20 major projects dealing with sheet-metal stamping, spot welding of galvanized steel, spinning of wheel disks, grinding of brake rotors, and molding and assembly bonding of plastic parts.

We have a simple formula for success with our Taguchi Methods training that I'd like to share: Our seminars are 5+1+2. We schedule a five-day off-site seminar conducted by the American Supplier Institute (ASI), Inc. The attendees are divided into product teams. These teams are subjected to classroom lecture, but they also initiate an experiment during the session. The team members continue this experiment at their respective divisions. Two months later, we have ASI consult on the experiment for one day at each of our divisions. In another two months, the teams return to an off-site location for two days, prepared to present the results of their experiment for critique.

We started with a small number of enthusiasts who attempted to carry the banner and promote the concept. I'll have to admit that there was a fair amount of skepticism among management and early students alike. Successful completion of case studies and application to actual product problems, however, has generated overwhelmingly positive attitudes.

Once we moved the concept out of the classroom and put it into practice, a creative and competitive interest took over that has resulted in at least 20 major project successes in less than a two-year period, as the following examples illustrate.

Our Stamping and Frame Division recently completed a study that investigated the relationship between press variables and stamping quality for the first draw-die operations on a door inner panel. Plans call for more experiments in the near future, with the ultimate goal being the routine use of Taguchi Methods during die tryout in order to provide quick determination of the optimum settings. This should improve our die transition times, as well as the consistency of our first-piece quality.

Another study within that division addressed the classic challenge of indirect spot welding of sheet-metal hem flanges. The challenge to which I'm referring is the maintenance of weld integrity while satisfying surface-appearance requirements. This was an interesting experiment for our people: You can assure either weld quality or surface quality at the expense of the other. Optimization of the process to satisfy both requirements was an experiment particularly well-suited for application of Taguchi Methods.

The end results were favorable in that we were able to reduce our internal repair and scrap costs significantly. It's also important to recognize, however, the improvement process involving this particular experiment. The experiment was initiated by a team of young engineers who were mechanically oriented but certainly not seasoned or even trained engineers. With five days of Taguchi Methods training, they went back to their plant to attempt to tell people in a company with 75 years of welding background how to improve. When the results proved favorable, the plant experts and skeptics were sure that their infinite job knowledge could have resolved the problem if someone had listened. Yes, job knowledge is important. In this case, however, Taguchi Methods provided the facts and discipline necessary to make sound judgments related to process changes. Moreover, the data were collected by hourly personnel, and the procedure was explained so that there wasn't idle involvement, but involvement with a degree of understanding.

Our Wheel and Brake Division reports success in applying Taguchi Methods to the manufacture of heavy truck wheels and the grinding and assembly of brake rotors. One study focusing on the assembly module for a large uni-cast rotor was designed to optimize eight control variables concerning five inspection characteristics. The results established control settings that reduced rework and scrap by 87.5%. Yet another study was aimed at determining process settings for a computer-numerically-controlled spinning machine that had been taken off-line because of poor performance. The experiment resulted in the machine's being placed back into production. That same machine is currently spinning wheel disks with a high degree of consistency.

Our Plastics Division has experienced similarly favorable results applying Taguchi Methods to the molding and assembly of automotive body panels, diesel-engine components, and water skis made of fiberglass-reinforced plastics. A recent study was aimed at minimizing the scrap rate of a molding process used to make an engine-valve cover. The experiment considered 14 process-control settings and four part characteristics that had been the cause of rejects in the past. The results identified control settings that may eliminate the incidence of one undesirable characteristic altogether and significantly reduce the recurrence of the others.

In addition to fine-tuning production processes so that they produce parts with less variability, Taguchi Methods provide other important benefits to The Budd Co.:

- They enhance communication between functional groups by providing a uniform communication format.
- They help the company determine the best methods of process control by rapidly determining the optimum setting for a number of control variables.
- They permit a more efficient method for changing processes, allowing fewer adjustments and more predictable effects from each adjustment.
- They reduce process costs with essentially no capital expenditures.
- They can be applied to a variety of processes.

When dealing with similar circumstances in the past, our people—while knowledgeable and dedicated—would tend to react to their gut feelings. Everyone would want to jump in and tear the machine or equipment apart without significant analysis of the problem. Taguchi Methods have allowed us to achieve a better understanding of process needs and requirements.

In the past, we would write procedures that were seldom read and almost never followed. Taguchi Methods have taught us to establish process parameters that are now set and controlled.

Analysis-of-Variance tables and Signal-to-Noise Ratios are terms familiar to practitioners of Taguchi Methods, but, frankly, they're foreign to me. Competition and the need for continuous planned improvement, however, aren't foreign to me or The Budd Co.

We see Taguchi Methods as a tool to improve the performance of a process as it's used in day-to-day production. I applaud ASI for its leadership in providing the technical expertise for—as well as a nontechnical understanding of—one of the ingredients in the pursuit of world-class quality.

. 5 .

Educating Today's Engineers

Robert H. Schaefer

Moving from a design-development process that's deterministic in nature to one that's statistically based is a journey our engineers must make. Approximately two years ago, the Chevrolet-Pontiac-Canada (C-P-C) Group of General Motors Corp. decided to embrace the concepts of Dr. Genichi Taguchi, and started formalizing plans for the implementation of his approach. Rather than dream up a strategy, we asked Dr. Taguchi for his advice on implementing these methods at C-P-C.

Dr. Taguchi said that we must do two things: use the case-study process and develop resident consultants. We did what he said and it appears to be working very well. I'd like to share with you the details of our strategy for implementing the Taguchi approach and the roadblocks and cultural issues we encountered and how we handled them.

Our implementation strategy isn't brilliant; as a matter of fact, it's fairly straightforward. It's basically a

Robert H. Schaefer is Reliability Engineering Director, Product Assurance and Validation, Chevrolet-Pontiac-Canada Group, General Motors Corp., Warren, Michigan.

43

three-pronged approach: the team case-study process, the resident Taguchi consultants, and the Taguchi Council.

Let's begin with the team case-study process. Taguchi Methods are taught through team training. Our teams are cross-functional and generally consist of five or more people. Most often, the teams are made up of engineers: design/development engineers, analytical engineers, manufacturing engineers, and engineers from our suppliers. But the teams aren't limited to engineers. We also include technicians and anyone else who can contribute to the project. Each team is required to bring a qualified real-life project to class. Team members receive 40 hours of training over several weeks, which gives them time between classes to gather data and work on the project. A resident Taguchi consultant is assigned to each team to help it through the rough spots. We try to make each case study a success.

Dr. Taguchi also told us that management must facilitate the case-study process. What that means is that management must participate in discussions with the teams and recognize them for their efforts. Bob Schultz, C-P-C Group Vice President, and his staff review one case study each month. This provides several benefits. It's an excellent way for top management to learn the benefits of the Taguchi approach, and staff members learn the language and learn to ask the right questions. It's also an excellent way to recognize the team, and it lets the work force know that top management is interested.

In August of 1986, C-P-C held its first symposium. Both C-P-C and corporate leaders participated. That symposium, like ASI's annual Taguchi symposium, was very motivational. It gave our case-study process a real shot in the arm. People tell us that we're lucky to have top-management support. Well, it wasn't that way in the beginning. We had to *earn* their support. How did we do it? With case studies that solved significant problems and yielded substantial savings. Several success stories were all it took.

The second element of the three-pronged approach is the resident Taguchi consultants. These consultants are the stars of earlier case studies. In addition to their regular jobs, these people work with the newly formed teams.

All of us at one time or another have gone to a class on a technical subject. After the class was over, we went back to our jobs and attempted to put into practice what we learned. What seemed so simple in class was no longer simple: It was complex and we needed help. This is precisely the time when an expert is required. Our resident Taguchi consultants help the team by questioning its approach, making suggestions, and even assisting with data analysis. We've found that the consultants' contributions are invaluable. In addition to working with the teams, the consultants perform on-the-job training with their peers. This allows us to go beyond the case-study process itself in spreading the use of the Taguchi approach.

Dr. Taguchi suggested that an optimum ratio of consultants to peers is 1:20. By the end of 1987, C-P-C had 1:100, and by the end of 1989, we hope to achieve the 1:20 ratio.

Figure 5–1 shows how we track the expertise levels of our engineers. In this example, a test engineer, Bill Biondo, is the resident Taguchi consultant for his chas-

Expertise Summary
Chassis Systems Development and Validation

	Taguchi	Weibull	Accel. Exp.	Rel. Growth	Root Cause	QFD (optional)	SPC (optional)
Awotwi, Samuel	⊕	◖	⊕	⊕	◖	⊕	⊕
Bejcak, Sally	⊕	◖	◖	⊕	◖	⊕	⊕
Biondo, Bill	●	⊕	⊕	⊕	⊕	⊕	◖
Bovac, Terry	⊕	⊕	⊕	⊕	⊕	⊕	⊕
Buescher, Larry	⊕	⊕	⊕	⊕	⊕	⊕	⊕
Bunge, Luke	⊕	⊕	⊕	⊕	⊕	⊕	⊕
Carroll, Glenn	⊕	⊕	⊕	⊕	⊕	⊕	⊕
Engelson, Eric	⊕	◖	◖	⊕	⊕	⊕	⊕
Gabrielson, Jim	⊕	⊕	⊕	⊕	⊕	⊕	⊕
Houshalter, Mark	⊕	⊕	⊕	⊕	⊕	⊕	⊕
Macciomei, Mike	⊕	⊕	⊕	⊕	⊕	⊕	⊕
Massos, Pete	⊕	⊕	⊕	⊕	⊕	⊕	⊕
Phillips, Ed	⊕	⊕	⊕	⊕	⊕	⊕	⊕
Purify, Esther	⊕	◖	◖	◖	⊕	⊕	◖
Rinke, Gordy	⊕	⊕	⊕	⊕	⊕	⊕	⊕
Yanssens, Jeff	⊕	◖	⊕	⊕	⊕	⊕	⊕
Ideal Profile	⊕	⊕	⊕	⊕	⊕	⊕	⊕

● = Teaches subject   ⊕ = Aware of subject

◖ = Consults on subject   ⊕ = No knowledge of subject

⊕ = Working knowledge

Figure 5–1. C-P-C uses an expertise summary to track the training level of its engineers in various quality methods. The third engineer on the list, Bill Biondo, is a resident Taguchi consultant.

sis test group. He spends approximately 50% of his time consulting with his peers in the test community. He also helps with the case-study teams. Bill wasn't singled out or chosen for this task. He, like all the other consultants, stepped forward because of interest and requested training. That's how it starts.

The third part of our implementation strategy is the Taguchi Council. The Council is made up of people who understand and have used Taguchi Methods. These people are the true believers, the fire-in-the-belly people. They're not appointees. They come from many areas within C-P-C—from engineering to the factory floor. The Council orchestrates the implementation process. It selects the teams to be trained and establishes the training criteria, which is tough. For every ten teams that apply for training, on the average only one is chosen.

This is a hard-nosed approach. But we're interested in quality, not quantity; successes, not failures. The Council also assigns the resident Taguchi consultants to the teams. Many feel that it's the dedication of this core group of people that has provided the real stimulus to our process.

And there you have it, a simple yet effective process. But what about the problems? We do indeed have our roadblocks—we're no different from anyone else. **Figure 5-2**, a flower picture borrowed from a bulletin board in a Japanese factory, illustrates these roadblocks. Workers at Diesel Kiki explained that this flower will grow very well on its own. All it takes is a little sunshine.

Figure 5-3, the flower picture redrawn, illustrates an important point. In this figure, the sun is management and the flowers are the successful use of new methods by the work force. The sunshine the flowers require

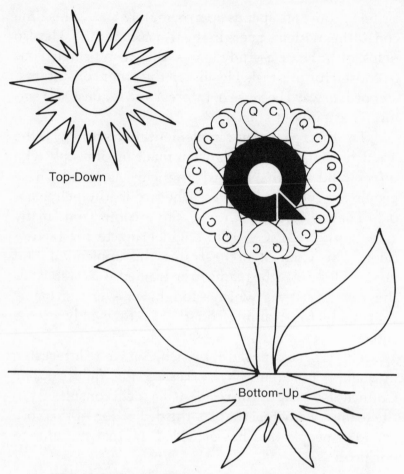

Top-Down

Bottom-Up

Figure 5–2. This flower picture borrowed from a Japanese bulletin board illustrates that flowers (successful use of new methods by the work force) grow well with a little sunshine (management support).

is for management to show support, ask the right questions, and provide recognition. With that, you'd think that the flowers would grow well. Not necessarily so.

Somewhere in every organization is a manager who

Top-Down
● Management must show
  visible support
● Management must constantly
  ask the right questions
● Management must provide
  recognition

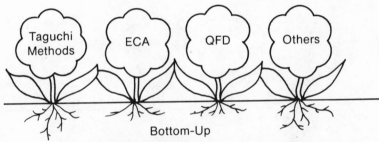

Figure 5–3. If management shows visible support, asks the right questions, and provides recognition, the flowers (successful use of new methods by the work force) should continue to grow.

insists on stomping on the flowers, as **Figure 5-4** shows. There are many reasons for this. When things are hot, it's difficult to free engineers for education and training—there's just too much to do. Or, it's OK for my engineers to go to class, but don't ask me stop a test or shut down the line to get data for that case study. Or more basic yet, "I don't want my people using that stuff in *my* area." In addition to these three reasons, there are at least 100 other ways to crush the flowers.

Why do managers do this? Thomas Jefferson once

Top-Down

Manager
- No time for class
- No time to gather case-study data
- Prohibit use of methods

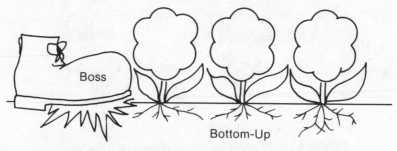

Boss

Bottom-Up

Figure 5–4. Unfortunately, every organization has at least one manager who insists on stomping on the flowers.

asked, "Why is it that men of goodwill insist on destroying that which they don't understand?" And there's our clue: If a manager doesn't understand a subject, chances are that he'll kill it. That's human nature, a fact of life. But could the reverse also be true? Our experience is that it is. If a manager understands a subject, chances are that he'll support it.

So, how do we get managers to understand? Here are three suggestions:

1. Require management overviews. This is one of

the few times that mandatory training is effective and necessary.

2. Have management teach. The cascade effect is a lot easier said than done. If done effectively, however, the results are extremely good.
3. Use the appraisal process to evaluate the manager on the genuine effort made to get himself and his people trained. The appraisal process is controversial, but if you have one use it for this purpose.

There are many other ideas on how to gain management support, but this should get the point across.

Of equal concern is the debating that occurs within an organization over the validity of one technical approach versus another. Debating casts a shadow and inhibits growth. Workers and management don't need this internal confusion. My advice is to take whatever steps are necessary to eliminate or minimize this problem. If left unchecked, it will undermine both efforts.

The following two points also apply to our implementation strategy. First, we believe in the "quality lever" (see **Figure 5-5**). Having the engineers apply the Taguchi approach during the design/development phases yields substantial return-on-investment rewards. Applying these methods during the production phase has its benefits. There's no doubt in our minds that the farther we push these methods upstream the greater the payoff. Desensitizing the design and finding potential problems during design and development are far less expensive than finding and fixing problems after tooling has been committed. We therefore emphasize the use of the Taguchi approach during the design and development phases.

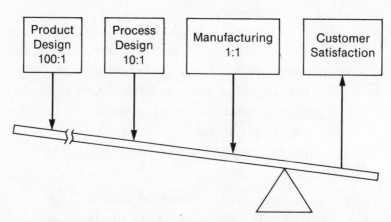

Figure 5–5. Applying quality technologies as far upstream as possible will provide the greatest payoff. Thus, C-P-C emphasizes the use of Taguchi Methods during design and development.

Second, the day-to-day jobs of our engineers are extremely demanding. The time it takes to educate and train these engineers is time taken away from the demands of their jobs, as noted earlier. C-P-C has dealt with this problem in several ways. There are those managers who understand and are 100% supportive. Most of these managers have had the mandatory overviews. They find the time for their people to be trained. The Taguchi Council looks to these groups for case studies. We also find that not all engineers are under the gun. For instance, the analytical and test engineers are generally more available for the application of these methods than the release engineers. By targeting our areas, we're more assured of achieving successful results. And as our successes mount, resistance crumbles.

The process described here is nearly two years old

and gaining momentum. Although we're far from where we'd like to be, the process is working very well. All too often we see processes come and go. It's no surprise when the troops say, "Here's another one of those programs." But we don't hear any of that about the case-study process.

Our Taguchi Council is presently tracking 80 to 90 case studies. Recently, case studies started appearing from areas that we hadn't any idea were using the methods. If you get more than you ask for, you can feel pretty good about the process that's been set in place. Is the process self-sustaining? Not yet—we need the 1:20 ratio of resident Taguchi consultants. Then it *will* be.

. 6 .

Specialists and Taguchi Methods

Dr. Don Clausing

Editor's Note: *The following essay is based on extemporaneous comments made at the Fifth Annual Taguchi Symposium, held October 8–9, 1987, in Detroit, Michigan. These comments followed the presentation made by Robert J. Schaefer of General Motors Corp., "Educating Today's Engineers."*

Larry Sullivan: How do we deal with statistical specialists and the ongoing debate that tends to paralyze management into doing nothing? This question comes up time and time again. Dr. Don Clausing of the Massachusetts Institute of Technology has experienced this problem personally; he has done a lot of consulting in the industry on Taguchi Methods. He has a very good perspective on the problem, the dangers of the problem, and how to solve the problem.

Dr. Clausing: I'd like to start out by congratulating

Dr. Don Clausing is Bernard M. Gordon Adjunct Professor of Engineering Innovation and Practice at Massachusetts Institute of Technology, Cambridge, Massachusetts. He was previously Manager and then Principal Engineer in the Advanced Development Activities at Xerox Corp.

Bob Schaefer not only for his presentation, but for the work that's gone into making the presentation possible, including all the management arrangements he described. I had the pleasure of visiting with Bob about a year and a half ago when C-P-C was still fairly new to these activities, and it's really gratifying to see the progress that's been made. In respect to the question of specialists, I think Bob already has the final answer: get rid of them. It sounds a bit draconian, but I think it's probably the only effective thing to do, particularly if people want to be argumentative, disputatious, disruptive, and not helpful. At some point you have to decide that it just isn't going to work and find some other place for them.

One of the most important of Dr. Taguchi's methods is parameter design, for both product design and production processes. When I was working at Xerox Corp. in the late 1970s, we had developed our own form of parameter design. We didn't *call* it parameter design, but that's what it was. It was a method of stress testing and operating windows. In 1980, we first encountered Taguchi Methods through the "Blue Book" (*Introduction to Off-Line Quality Control*) by Dr. Taguchi and Professor Yuin Wu. I read with great interest the first three or four chapters on the Quality Loss Function, and I said, "Boy, this is really powerful stuff; this guy Taguchi is apparently onto something here." And then I got to the Wheatstone Bridge (a type of electrical circuit) case-study example of parameter design, and I couldn't understand it. There were some problems and misprints in the equations in the book, which didn't help much. So I put the book aside and said, "It looks powerful but I can't understand it—someday I'll have to try and figure it out."

In 1982, I had the pleasure and opportunity of meeting and talking to Dr. Taguchi, and I started to understand that what he called parameter design was what we were already doing. He had it much more highly developed, however, and it was much more efficient than what we were doing. But our form of parameter design had proven highly effective and made dramatic improvements over the old, haphazard, one-factor-at-a-time experimentation. Once I understood that Dr. Taguchi's method was better, I thought it was a really good thing; I began to implement it, and for the past five years have been helping people do the same. In a recent interview in a Japanese journal, Dr. Taguchi talks about the application of Taguchi Methods and the origin of the name, for which I seem to have gotten the blame; in my more formal moments, however, I call it "Quality Engineering at Low Cost."

When we set out to implement Taguchi Methods, we found some problems—and there are a lot of problems. Bob has done an excellent job of addressing them. I'll just add a few comments. One of the problems is that people, specifically engineers and statisticians, tend to react in a very specialized way; let's focus on engineers. Engineers will probably react to any new method, but in regard to Taguchi Methods, they tend to react as if they were a theorem in geometry. You remember proving a theorem in geometry: If you could show any counterexample, it proved that the whole theorem was no good, and you would just throw the theorem out. That's all right for a theorem in geometry, but a lot of engineers want to use that same approach with new methods. All methods are going to have some problem in application: They're going to look like they don't work on some particular case study somewhere, sometime. If we take the Euclidean geometric-theorem-proving approach, we can just say it didn't work, so let's throw it out. If it doesn't work 100% every time, it can't be very good; let's not do it. To some extent, that's just a defense mechanism for the desire not to change in the first place. To the extent that it has some intellectual basis, it's an attempt to apply this Euclidean-theorem approach to methodology.

There's been some really brilliant research done on this general subject—how do we implement improvements and how do we think about them?—by Joel Moses of MIT and Rosabeth Kanter of the Harvard Business School. Moses points out that in the United States, and in the Western world in general, we tend to want methods that are general, methods that we can be confident will work every time. The problem with such methods is that they usually do so because they're not being used to do very much, and they aren't really very powerful. On the other hand, methods that are really powerful and accomplish a great deal aren't totally general. The beauty and power of them are that they work nearly all the time in situations that are really important. So a method is good if it will produce outstanding results in 95% of the cases. The fact that it may not produce outstanding results in the other 5% is OK. We have to get away from this specialized-knowledge, geometry-theorem approach. Approached in this way, Taguchi Methods aren't going to work every time, and we shouldn't argue about the fact that there are occasions where they don't work so well. Even in those cases, we probably just need to apply them better.

Beyond that, there's the question of the role of statisticians and engineers in all of this. I'll try not to make this my usual diatribe against statisticians. Statisticians are fine people. There are, however, some problems in the way that engineers and statisticians interact. Being an engineer, I tend to attribute these problems in my more informal moments to some problem with statisticians. But it takes two in this kind of situation to have a problem. In some ways, from a historical perspective it seems like we're repeating history.

In fact, at the turn of the century there was the new operational mathematics of Oliver Heaviside in Great Britain. Heaviside was an electrical engineer. He started doing these operational transforms and the mathematicians were all bent out of shape because the transforms were all wrong, he hadn't proven a lot of things, and so forth. But the transforms were very effective in electrical engineering. And so this battle went on for some time. Heaviside just kind of ignored it and went on successfully doing his thing, and the mathematicians went on being unhappy. Finally, some of them stopped arguing about it and started trying to prove that he was wrong, and when they did they found that he was right. (Heaviside later said that even Cambridge mathematicians should be given justice.)

So we have to keep it all in perspective: Even if we can't prove something 100% mathematically, it still may be very good; at the same time, we don't want to get too upset with people who are saying that it's no good because they haven't gotten around to proving that it's all right.

With respect to the role of statisticians and engineers, let me try to give a balanced view at this point. Another thing that comes out of the research by Moses and Kanter is that in the U.S. we tend to be too segmented. For example, we have engineers in one segment and statisticians in another segment, and these two segments don't talk much to each other, certainly not effectively. And it's not just engineers and statisticians: It's design engineers and production people, product planners and design engineers. We're segmented in many ways. The segmentation of statisticians and engineers, however, has a great bearing on the topic of developing better methods for optimizing products and production processes. Now as I said, at Xerox we had developed a form of parameter design. It didn't have any statistics in it, and for that reason it wasn't very efficient, but it was dramatically successful simply because the objective of parameter design is itself so powerful. We engineers had developed a powerful methodology, but it still wasn't as effective as it should have been by any means—although it was a lot more effective than the traditional poke-and-hope kind of approach.

By 1979, I had concluded that we needed to bring some statistics into the design to make it more efficient, and we started trying to do that. So we had the right objective—parameter design; i.e., reducing variance to make products work well under a wide range of circumstances. But we didn't really have the detailed statistical techniques we needed to make it more effective. The statisticians, on the other hand—and not being a statistician I can only characterize what they did with some concern—had developed a lot of techniques, but with respect to what's important in the economics and engineering of products and production processes, they really hadn't come across the right objectives. The objective of parameter design wasn't being worked on by the statistical technicians at all. I just want to leave it at that—just with the idea that the engineers and the statisticians were overly segmented.

If I as an engineer had been paying more attention to what the statisticians were doing, or if the statisticians had been paying more attention to what engineers such as myself were doing to develop parameter design—if we'd not been so segmented and had gotten together to work effectively—we'd have probably ended up where Dr. Taguchi has been for at least ten years now. Which is to say that Dr. Taguchi didn't get boxed into these separate segmental traps; instead he did broad thinking across engineering and statistical lines and integrated these lines together to get the most effective techniques with the right objectives. We remained excessively segmented, and I'll take my part of the blame as an engineer for not looking at statistics sufficiently. And I would suggest to the statisticians that they take *their* part of the blame for not looking at engineering and economic objectives sufficiently and that we stop having arguments that, in the long run, aren't at all effective.

In reality, if people are going to keep on with such arguments, the only solution that effective managers can implement is the one that Bob Schaefer suggested. So I'd suggest that the real problem isn't that as an engineer I shouldn't blame the statisticians, or that the statisticians shouldn't blame the engineers; rather, it is probably fundamental to our overly-segmented culture. One group in this segment, another group in that segment; we didn't get together and do the kind of broad, integrated thinking that was needed to achieve the right techniques and the right objectives. Dr. Taguchi *did*, and that's why most of us are trying to use his methods in the most effective way possible.

.7.

Quality Function
Deployment

Dr. Don Clausing

In March 1984, I had the opportunity to discuss new product development with Dr. Hajime Makabe of the Tokyo Institute of Technology while visiting Fuji-Xerox Ltd. Dr. Makabe explained that while he still taught and consulted on some traditional subjects, the really important material was Quality Function Deployment (QFD), a product-development tool that systematically deploys customer requirements into production requirements that guide production operations on the factory floor. As he described QFD and its success in Japanese industry, I became increasingly excited: It was apparent that QFD would help overcome serious problems in product development and production in U.S. manufacturing.

As a result of that initial discussion, some ensuing observations of consultations by Dr. Makabe with Fuji-Xerox people, and other discussions at Fuji-Xerox regarding implementation of QFD, I returned to the

---

Dr. Don Clausing is Bernard M. Gordon Adjunct Professor of Engineering Innovation and Practice at Massachusetts Institute of Technology, Cambridge, Massachusetts. He was previously Manager and then Principal Engineer in the Advanced Development Activities of Xerox Corp.

63

United States and started lectures and private conversations to help American industry benefit from the process. This led to an explosion of interest and activity in QFD in the automotive industry.

QFD's primary goal is the overcoming of three major problems: disregard for the voice of the customer, loss of information, and different individuals and functions working to different requirements. The ultimate benefits of QFD are increased market share and larger profits. These benefits are realized because QFD plays a major role in achieving products that have reduced costs, improved quality, features that satisfy customer needs, and significantly shorter development times. As a result, the products are intrinsically much more appealing to potential customers and sell themselves without such special sales measures as reduced interest rates.

What Is QFD?

QFD consists of two things: well-developed formats and a style of organizational behavior that facilitates a holistic response to customer needs. The formats—matrices and charts that have been developed on the basis of experience over the past 16 years—guide the work and provide for easy, standardized documentation during product development and production.

The matrices and charts create a flowchart for the important product-development activities that lead to production: product planning, design, process planning, and production planning. The formats also help ensure that work is properly documented in a form that's easily recognizable and understandable by everyone in the organization. For example, machine operators can trace

any specific production operation back through the series of charts that are summarized in **Figure 7-1** and see
exactly how the operation helps achieve the needed part
characteristics, which help meet the design requirements, which, in turn, are responsive to customer
requirements.

Figure 7-1 illustrates the basic structure of QFD.
It's convenient to think of QFD as consisting of four activities. In the product-planning activity, customer requirements are deployed into product-expectation characteristics and specifications that then become design
requirements. In the design activity (parts deployment),
the design requirements established during product
planning are deployed through the concept and design

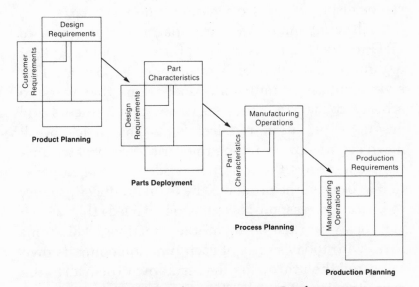

*Figure 7-1. Quality Function Deployment
charts and matrices deploy customer requirements and related technical requirements all
the way down to the factory floor.*

activity to become part characteristics (e.g., dimensions). In the process-planning activity, part characteristics are deployed into manufacturing operations (production processes) that will achieve the required part characteristics. Then, in the production-planning activity, manufacturing operations are deployed into detailed production requirements to enable production operations on the factory floor to achieve all the required production processes.

Although **Figure 7-1** shows QFD as four activities, it would be extremely segmentalist for us to think of them as four independent activities: They must all be closely integrated. In particular, design (parts deployment) and process planning must be done as one integrated activity. The output from this activity, however, can be displayed on two separate summary charts.

Although much of the initial attention given to QFD in the U.S. focused on its formats, QFD's style of organizational behavior is even more important. This style emphasizes multifunctional teams that work to achieve consensus about customer requirements and product-expectation requirements. This helps break down segmentation among the various corporate functions and brings the collective wisdom of the corporation to bear on the product. The team produces product specifications responsive to customer needs that will be vigorously worked on by all the functions. This compares with today's style of each function doing its own thing and then throwing the result over the wall to the next function. The multifunctional team for the first phase of QFD, product planning, usually includes representatives from product planning, marketing, market research, design, production processes, production operations, service, and, very likely, finance and purchasing.

Why Do We Need QFD?

Perhaps the need for QFD can be most dramatically recognized by comparing today with the past, before the Industrial Revolution. Roughly 400 years ago, when a knight went to an armorer to discuss a new suit of armor, the two men would achieve consensus about the armor's specifications and design features. For example, they agreed that the armor would be plate armor, not chain armor. Next, the armorer translated (deployed) these specifications into design details. For example, he decided that the armor should have fluted surfaces to achieve greater bending strength for the plates. Of course, such a major decision as this would be verified with the knight. Then, the armorer translated these design details into production processes that would achieve the required design characteristics. For example, the armorer decided that the steel plates should be quenched in black goat urine to achieve proper hardness of the steel. Lastly, the armorer translated the production processes into detailed production planning. For example, he decided that the forge fire needed to be lit at 6 a.m. in order to achieve a sufficient temperature to properly heat-treat the armor.

The main point of this little historical vignette is that the deployment of the armor's required features and characteristics was quite simple; it was all done by two men, the customer and the manufacturer. Most of the deployment was actually done in the armorer's head, where he had all the specialized technical knowledge of the day.

If we carried the deployment style used by the knight and the armorer into today's world, we would have customers on the factory floor talking to machine operators in order to deploy customer needs. We can immediately see that the simple deployment style of 400 years ago is totally inadequate in today's highly sophisticated manufacturing environment. Today, we have many corporate specialists who are knowledgeable about the tremendous amount of specialized technical knowledge that's been acquired during the last 400 years. This specialized knowledge has provided substantial benefits to customers in the form of improved products. It has also created considerable problems in the development and production processes.

There's a tendency for specialists to stay cloistered within their specialties. Individually, they contribute tremendous specialized knowledge, but there's some difficulty in integrating that knowledge so that it provides a holistic response to customer needs. By analogy with the knight and the armorer, we can think of our job as being primarily to help customers talk to machine operators. We must develop improved multifunctional integration so that we can help these two groups talk to each other, while at the same time bringing into play our reservoir of specialized knowledge.

The need for QFD is illustrated by the corporate communication circle of **Figure 7-2**. There's an old party game in which the guests are arranged in a circle. One person whispers a short anecdote to the neighbor on his or her left, and the story is whispered around the circle

Corporate Communication Circle

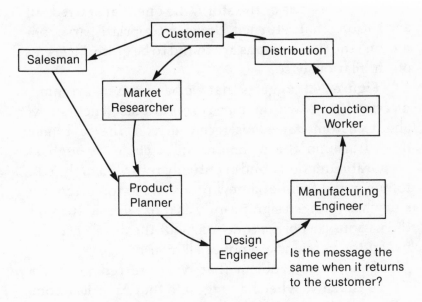

Example: English to Russian to English Translation

"The spirit is willing, but the flesh is weak."
becomes
"The wine is o.k., but the meat is rotten."

Conclusion: Make sure customers receive their quality requirements: Don't let the corporate communication circle translate customer quality requirements into rotten meat.

Figure 7–2. Customer needs are passed around the corporate communication circle and returned to the customer in the form of a new product. All too often, however, customer needs don't get properly translated from department to department. QFD keeps this from happening.

until it returns to the original teller. This person then tells both versions of the story, the one that started out and the one that returned. Under appropriate party conditions, the two versions are found to be quite different, often hilariously so.

Figure 7-2 suggests that we have a similar communication circle within our corporations. The "story" about customer needs is received from the customer, passed around the communication circle through all corporate functions, and eventually returned to the customer in the form of a new product. All too often, the story has changed significantly as it has passed through the various corporate functions, but the differences between the versions are not at all hilarious.

This is the problem that was referred to by Dr. Kaoru Ishikawa when he suggested that American companies need stronger horizontal orientations to provide a strong cross-functional fabric. The problem can be further understood by considering the simple two-step translation of a well-known English aphorism into a foreign language: "The spirit is willing, but the flesh is weak" becomes "The wine is o.k., but the meat is rotten." One can easily see that this might happen. It's exactly the same problem that we're concerned with in the corporate communication circle. The difference in language between two major corporate functions isn't as great as the difference between English and a foreign language, but it's nevertheless substantial. Differences in language, knowledge, experience, and values among corporate functions are great enough to cause significant problems. This appears to be natural and inherent in the way we're organized and do business. A disciplined, structured methodology is needed to help overcome this natural dysfunction. It was this observation that led to the development of QFD in Japan.

The problem of weak horizontal orientation is even more profound than the difficulties it presents in moving new products through the various corporate functions. As illustrated in **Figure 7–3**, we can think of the problems and opportunities in terms of a structure of five rings. As we move outward, each ring represents an increasingly more profound cause. The "five why's" appear rooted in Japanese folklore. If we ask why once and get a good answer, we haven't reached the bottom of the question. The Japanese have determined on the basis of experience that asking five why's will yield some sort of ultimate truth or definition of the most fundamental cause. Applying this thinking to our current situation in manufacturing provides the concept shown in the figure. The third ring shows that QFD, Company-Wide Quality Control (CWQC), Taguchi Methods, and Just-in-Time (JIT, Toyota's production system) have a profound effect on achieving Japanese-made products that appeal to customers. Why did these improved practices grow up in Japan rather than elsewhere? Recent research suggests that stronger horizontal orientation enables greater flexibility and facilitates the implementation of improved practices. This suggests that our weak horizontal orientation also makes it difficult for us to implement improvements in our methods.

When specialists polish their own specialties within their own segments, their activities may appear very elegant and impressive. But all too often, they simply lead to "institutionalization of waste." An example of institutionalization of waste is high-bay (vertical) automated storage and retrieval systems (AS/RS), which have

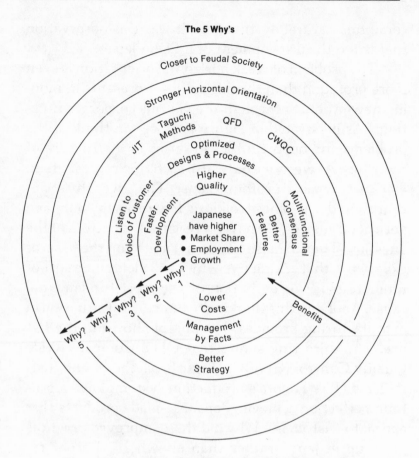

Figure 7–3. The "five why's" concept can be applied to the status of U.S. manufacturing. The third ring shows that Quality Function Deployment (QFD), Taguchi Methods, Company-Wide Quality Control (CWQC), and Just-in-Time (JIT) production have a profound effect on achieving products that appeal to customers.

become quite fashionable in the last ten years. Given that the objective is to store and retrieve inventory, these systems appear to be an elegant and impressive solution developed by specialists in material management. In Toyota's JIT system, however, the objective isn't to more elegantly store and retrieve inventory, but to *minimize* inventory. Thus, the high-bay AS/RS have institutionalized waste in the form of excessive inventory and the quality problems that it hides. A leading American JIT implementer has noted that once we move on to improved practice of JIT, about all we'll be able to do with these systems is take a bulldozer to them.

QFD can certainly help improve our horizontal orientation—particularly with respect to moving new products through the various corporate functions—and thus may also help overcome the problem of institutionalization of waste.

Implementation and Benefits

What can executives do to help capture the benefits of QFD? Some challenges never change. The tendency to resist the implementation of improvements seems to be invariant with time. Consider the following statement made by Machiavelli more than 400 years ago: "It must be considered that there is nothing more difficult to carry out, nor more doubtful of success, nor more dangerous to handle, than to initiate a new order of things. For the reformer has enemies in all those who profit by the old order, and only lukewarm defenders in all those who would profit by the new order, this lukewarmness arising partly from fear of their adversaries, who have the laws in their favour; and partly from the incredulity of mankind, who do not truly believe in any-thing new until they have had actual experience of it. Thus it arises that on every opportunity for attacking the reformer, his opponents do so with zeal of partisans, the others only defend him half-heartedly, so that be-tween them he runs great danger."

To paraphrase Machiavelli, when important im-provements are available there will inevitably be those who advocate them and those who tend to resist them because the risk seems too great to them personally. Those who are concerned about the risk tend to be more dynamic in their risk aversion than the proponents of change, who inevitably aren't sure of their ground. Therefore, there's some bias in the dynamics of human interaction in favor of the status quo.

What can be done to overcome this natural bias against the implementation of improvement? During his visit to the U.S. in 1986, Dr. Shigeru Mizuno, in many ways the father of QFD, said that after a Japanese company had some experience with QFD, its president proclaimed that the company wanted to be number one in the world in its business, and in order to be number one, the company must use QFD. Leaders must provide strong direction or change will not occur. It's easy to ob-serve why this is so. Inevitably in the introduction of some important new way of doing business, there will come a time of uncertainty and doubt, and there may be some setbacks before the benefits have been totally demonstrated. At this point, it's easy for the new meth-od to collapse, but with executive leadership there will be sufficient determination and perseverance to over-come these dark moments before the dawn. As American statistician Dr. W. Edwards Deming noted, "Constancy of purpose is required."

Beyond proclaiming that the company must use QFD, executives might consider other measures to improve the integration that overcomes segmentalist tendencies. One major improvement is to change the reward system to favor more holistic responses to current challenges. An obvious example is to put more emphasis on the rewarding of teams. This can lead fairly directly to improved teamwork. Another example is to put more emphasis on input from other functions in evaluating the work in order to determine appropriate rewards, which will help overcome institutionalization of waste. If the work appears elegant to other specialists within that segment of the corporation, it will inevitably be regarded as deserving of a positive reward. In cases of institutionalization of waste, however, the activity often appears elegant to the specialists of the segment, but people in other functions may not discern adequate output in response to customer needs. A more balanced perspective can be achieved by inclusion of input from other functions regarding the value of the work that's been done.

In summary, QFD carries the voice of the customer to the factory floor. It brings all the corporate wisdom, including all the specialized knowledge of the many and diverse corporate specialists, to bear on the product. And it achieves multifunctional consensus, which results in a product that's best for the customer and the corporation. QFD is a major operational practice that helps achieve products that are higher in quality, lower in cost, and developed much faster, and that contain features that are better matched to customer requirements. By using QFD to achieve products that strongly appeal to potential customers, corporations will experience increased market share and growth and improved quality of work life.

. 8 .

QFD and You

William E. Eureka and Nancy E. Ryan

It's time to update the old widget story. Imagine this: Your company has just introduced a new widget— at half the cost and twice the productivity and quality of the competition's widgets, and in two-thirds the time. Contributing to this feat was Quality Function Deployment (QFD)—a system for translating customer requirements into appropriate technical requirements at each stage of the product-development process—and the engineering tools it specifies.

Half the cost and twice the productivity and quality in two-thirds the time—that's what QFD helps achieve, as the following real-life example illustrates. Toyota Motor Corp.'s primary transmission supplier, Aisin Warner, a subsidiary of Aisin Seiki Co., Ltd., Kariya, Japan, used QFD to reduce the number of engineering changes during product development by half. Development time and start-up cycles were also cut in half, enhancing the overall time to market. Numerous other

This chapter is excerpted from *The Customer-Driven Company: Managerial Perspectives on QFD*, published by the ASI Press. William E. Eureka is Vice President and General Manager of the American Supplier Institute, Inc., Dearborn, Michigan. Nancy E. Ryan is a member of the ASI Press.

Japanese companies are using QFD to similar avail. They are—or soon will be—your competition.

What exactly is QFD? George R. Perry, Vice President, Quality and Reliability, Allied-Signal, Inc., Southfield, Michigan, defines QFD as "a systematic way of ensuring that the development of product features, characteristics, and specifications, as well as the selection and development of process equipment, methods, and controls, are driven by the demands of the customer or marketplace."

QFD is a system for translating customer requirements into appropriate company requirements at each stage of the product-development cycle, from research and development to engineering, manufacturing, marketing, sales, and distribution (see **Figure 8–1**).

Taken literally, the term Quality Function Deployment may seem a bit misleading. QFD isn't a quality tool—although it can certainly improve quality in the broadest sense of the word. Rather, it's a visually powerful planning tool. And although first used by the Japanese, several aspects of QFD resemble Value Analysis/Value Engineering (VAVE), a process developed in America, combined with marketing techniques.

The term Quality Function Deployment is derived from six Chinese/Japanese characters: *hin shitsu* (qualities, features, or attributes), *ki no* (function), and *ten kai* (deployment, development, or diffusion), as **Figure 8–2** illustrates. The translation is inexact, as well as nondescriptive of the actual QFD process: *Hin shitsu* is synonymous with qualities (i.e., features or attributes), not quality.

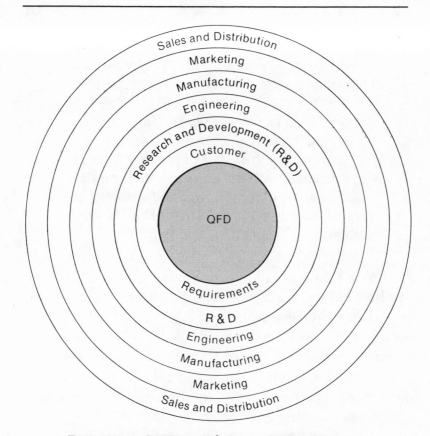

Figure 8–1. QFD translates customer requirements into appropriate company requirements at each stage of the product-development process.

Improved Product Development

QFD brings out the best in a variety of engineering tools already available, which, when properly applied, will help ensure quality products.

品質　機能　展開

Hin Shitsu	Ki No	Ten Kai
(Quality)	(Function)	(Deployment)

Figure 8–2. The term Quality Function Deployment is derived from six Chinese/Japanese characters: **hin shitsu** *(quality features or attributes),* **ki no** *(function), and* **ten kai** *(deployment, development, or diffusion). The translation is inexact:* **Hin shitsu** *is synonymous with qualities, not quality.*

With QFD, broad product-development objectives are broken down into specific, actionable assignments via a comprehensive team effort. Without this team approach, QFD loses much of its power. The process is accomplished via a series of matrices and charts that deploy customer requirements and related technical requirements from product planning and product design to process planning and the shop floor.

On a short-term basis, QFD results in fewer start-up problems, fewer design changes, and shorter product-development cycles—"must haves" for improved engineering productivity and reduced costs. Even more important, however, are such long-term benefits as satisfied customers, lower warranty costs, and increased market share.

When the process is correctly utilized, it creates a closed loop consisting of ever-improving cost, quality, and timeliness; productivity and profitability; and market share. Each of these elements figures prominently in QFD; together, these elements equate to competitive strength—competitive strength that the Japanese are now enjoying (see **Figure 8-3**).

Competitive Strength from QFD

Figure 8-3. The use of QFD results in improved cost, quality, and timeliness, which result in increased productivity and profitability and, ultimately, market share.

The first QFD matrix, the "House of Quality," serves as the basis for subsequent QFD phases. The information provided in this initial QFD phase is used to identify specific design requirements that must be achieved in order to satisfy customer requirements. [The mechanics of the total QFD process are reviewed at greater length in Chapter 2 of *The Customer-Driven Company*.]

QFD is not a high technology; rather, it's a medium-to-low technology based on common sense. QFD does, however, have a place in the high-tech realm: Efficient information transfer is as important, or perhaps even more important, with high-technology processes as it is with more traditional technologies.

QFD can lead to effective technology generation in response to customer requirements. This results in technology investments that add value to the products being manufactured, rather than technology investments that become expensive white elephants. Incremental implementation of new technology can please both coffers and customers.

As more and more companies are finding out, high tech isn't a panacea to be prescribed whenever market share dips, although it can certainly enhance product-development activities after strategic product planning has occurred.

Many American automotive plants have received high-tech facelifts in recent years, yet few have matched the quality and productivity attained at the joint GM/Toyota plant in Fremont, California—no factory of the future. The NUMMI (New United Motors Manufacturing, Inc.) plant is run by the Japanese but employs American workers, discounting the theory that Japanese manufacturing principles won't work in American industrial settings.

"We have to become good at what I call medium tech," explains Dr. Don Clausing, Bernard M. Gordon Adjunct Professor of Engineering Innovation and Practice at Massachusetts Institute of Technology, Cambridge, Massachusetts. "We tend to want to retrench to high technology because we feel it's where we still have an edge."

Clausing, previously Principal Engineer in the Advanced Development Activities of Xerox Corp., was introduced to QFD in March 1984 while visiting Fuji-Xerox Ltd., Tokyo, Japan. His research into the company's product-development process led to a meeting with one of its primary consultants, Dr. Hajime Makabe. After returning from Japan, Clausing shared his QFD knowledge with engineers from Ford Motor Co., Dearborn, Michigan.

Next came a series of annual American Supplier Institute (ASI), Inc., study missions to Japan that focused
increased attention on QFD. QFD has now taken off in
the United States—15 years after the methodology was
formalized at Kobe Shipyard, Mitsubishi Heavy Industries Ltd., Kobe, Japan.

Kobe Shipyard builds ships that are both massive
and sophisticated. Although the shipyard builds only
one such ship at a time, the potential benefits of a strategic planning system that details and documents the relationship between the quality of a finished product and
that product's components were not lost upon company
management.

Is such a system needed in the United States? Yes.
By addressing a fundamental weakness of Western society, lack of adequate planning, QFD can help us shore
up our weaknesses while building on our strengths. It
encourages a comprehensive, holistic approach to product development generally found lacking in American
industry.

Quality Defined

The majority of companies doing business in the
world today list "produce high-quality products" or
"provide high-quality service" as one of their foremost
goals. But what, precisely, is a high-quality product or
high-quality service? Ask the question more than once
and you'll surely get conflicting answers. And do high-
quality products always turn a profit? Obviously not.
More elementary yet, what exactly *is* quality? To some,
it's conformance to specification limits. To others, it's
much more.

Quality control, too, is subject to different interpretations. According to *Webster's Ninth New Collegiate Dictionary*, quality control is "an aggregate of activities (as design analysis and statistical sampling with inspection for defects) designed to ensure adequate quality, especially in manufactured products."

Another standard reference source, the *McGraw-Hill Dictionary of Scientific and Technical Terms*, prefers this definition: "inspection, analysis, and action applied to a portion of the product in a manufacturing operation to estimate overall quality of the product and determine what, if any, changes must be made to achieve or maintain the required level of quality."

"Glossary and Tables for Statistical Quality Control," published by the American Society for Quality Control, on the other hand, defines quality control as "the overall system of activities whose purpose is to provide a quality of product or service that meets the needs of users; also, the use of such a system."

The Japanese definition of quality control differs even more markedly. As recorded in Japan Industrial Standard Z8101–1981, "Quality control is a system of means to economically produce goods or services that satisfy customer requirements. Implementing quality control effectively necessitates the cooperation of all people in the company, involving top management, managers, supervisors, and workers in all areas of corporate activities, such as market research, research and development, product planning, design, preparations for production, purchasing, vendor management, manufacturing, inspection, sales and after services, as well as financial control, personnel administration, and training and education. Quality control carried out in this manner is called Company-Wide Quality Control."

In addition, the Japanese concept of quality appears to be more comprehensive than the characteristics usually associated with quality, encompassing performance, extra features (added options), reliability, durability, serviceability, aesthetics, and conformance to standards.

Like beauty, quality is in the eye of the beholder. The beholder, in the case of product-development activities, should be the customer. Hence, any definition of quality should be supplied by the customer—which is what QFD ensures. Quality, which is in the eye of the customer, is communicated via the "voice of the customer."

The Need for QFD

As consumers become more cost- and value-conscious, they're turning to alternative sources for products. Lucrative price incentives may temporarily appease these consumers and increase market share, but they aren't a viable long-term business approach. As competitors match price incentives, the net result is to lower the profit margin of the respective industrial sector.

These value-conscious consumers are demanding ever-improving levels of quality. When they don't get it, they go elsewhere. Also, a customer lost because of a quality problem may never return—and may take 20 or more other customers with him or her.

Time to market is increasingly critical for capturing market share: It's easier to capture market share by being first to market with a desirable product than to win customers back with a late entry. Companies with lengthy product-development cycles are especially vulnerable: Such product-development cycles make it extremely difficult to forecast market requirements. Reduced product-development cycles help companies more accurately match products to consumers and take the guesswork out of market forecasting.

Quality, cost, timeliness, and productivity are often viewed as conflicting elements that require the making of trade-offs. The best Japanese companies, however, have learned to successfully optimize these apparently conflicting objectives while making minimal trade-offs, achieving both increased market share and profits and loyal customer followings.

QFD has played an important part in this optimization, helping improve quality, timeliness, and productivity while reducing costs.

Focus: Problem Prevention

The best Japanese companies deploy the voice of the customer to help determine important product attributes. Engineers at these Japanese companies then design and build to target values, seeking to reduce manufacturing variation around these targets. The Japanese focus on optimizing the product and the process, not only to maximize performance but also to reduce variation. This results in consistent high performance, from product to product and throughout the product's lifetime.

By front-loading product-development efforts, the Japanese focus on planning and problem prevention, not

Problem Prevention

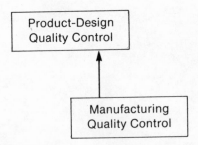

Figure 8–4. QFD results in an upstream, product-design-oriented—versus a downstream, manufacturing-oriented—form of quality control.

problem solving. QFD is one of the methodologies used to make the transition from reactive to preventive—from downstream, manufacturing-oriented quality control to upstream, product-design-oriented quality control (see **Figure 8-4**). It does so by defining "what to do" and "how to do it" in a manner that results in the consistent performance that satisfies customers.

By clearly defining the job objectives needed to achieve it, QFD helps build customer-defined quality into a product. While it doesn't *guarantee* success, QFD greatly improves the probability of achieving it. Without QFD, you get what you've always gotten. With it, you get a new, improved approach to product planning.

·9·

Putting QFD to Work

W. E. Scollard

About eight years ago, a Ford dealer gave me a very basic explanation of Quality Function Deployment (QFD). When I asked him what we had to do to sell cars, he said, "You've got to build them for the taker, not the maker." Of course, neither of us knew about QFD at the time. But essentially, that's what we expect QFD to do at Ford Motor Co. It will allow Ford and its suppliers to build cars for the takers, or customers.

Giving customers what they want isn't that simple. Our customers want quality, and we want to give it to them. All we have to do is deliver it. We start by defining quality. To paraphrase my dealer friend, "Quality has to be defined by the taker, not the maker." A technically flawless car isn't a quality car unless it meets customer needs. QFD is a powerful tool to help make sure we meet those needs.

Five years ago, our market-research department spent all its time and budget finding out how best to sell cars—*after* we built them. Now market research spends more than half its time and budget finding out what our

W. E. Scollard is Vice President of Manufacturing Operations, Ford Motor Co., Dearborn, Michigan.

customers like and dislike so we can make it part of our development process.

In the past, we used a similar approach in manufacturing. We were looking for quality after the fact—by working hard to fix problems. We call that the find-and-fix mode. I'm sure that many of you are familiar with it. It simply means that we wait for the customer to find a problem, and then we fix it. Find and fix is an expensive, time-consuming way to deliver quality. Worst of all, it doesn't really help us deliver quality to the customer. Instead, with find and fix we use the customer as an extension of our product-testing and quality-inspection system. Even then, we have a tendency to treat symptoms rather than the root cause.

A component supplier generally can't fix a problem in our design. And a design problem can't be fixed by a mechanic at a dealership. All they can do is treat symptoms that crop up in their particular area. If they create a problem for another area, that's the other area's problem.

In the find-and-fix mode, you never really solve anything. You never really get to the prevention of problems. Resources are wasted dealing with the same problems over and over again. The problems recur, and, in fact, they can go on indefinitely. Twenty-five years ago, I was a plant manager in what was then our General Parts Division. I now find that people are still fixing problems I'd tried to fix in 1962. But we didn't get to the root cause when we fixed something, and we didn't address prevention of the problem happening again.

QFD helps us find the heart of a problem. It requires that suppliers, designers, engineers, and production people communicate with each other and with end users. They work as a QFD team to trace problems to the source and deal with them once and for all. But most important, QFD helps *prevent* problems. By prevention, I mean dealing with issues at an early stage—designing the product and the process in a way that prevents problems that irritate customers. In addition, it calls our attention to the positive things that customers want, so we can design them in at the beginning. When QFD teams meet in the early stages of product development, they can flag trouble spots and deal with them efficiently.

Here are some specific examples of how QFD has been applied at Ford. I recently conducted a kind of grass-roots poll of the people at Ford who've used QFD. Quite honestly, we haven't been using QFD long enough to collect a lot of hard data. But that really isn't what I wanted. I wanted to get people's gut reaction to QFD. Do they view it as a powerful tool that can help Ford, or is it a buzzword, just another passing fad? Judging by their reactions, the term may fade—but that's because QFD will become a way of doing business.

One of the first applications of QFD at Ford was in developing the new Lincoln Continental. We're marketing it as a technically innovative car, because our market research told us that's what customers want in that segment of the market. From our work on the Taurus, we found that a key feature in this marketing strategy is variable-assist steering. Our engineers believe that we hit the target and that QFD is one of the reasons why.

Since we knew that customers wanted variable-assist steering, we addressed many different aspects of that feature. QFD helped us nail down the ones most important to our customers. This gets back to the old theory, "Don't fix what isn't broken." We didn't spend time on things our customers liked. Instead, we concentrated on areas they wanted improved. In some situations, our QFD findings showed gaps when engineering-specification test requirements were compared to customer requirements. The tests were then modified to meet customer needs and wants rather than the wants of our engineers—"Build it for the taker, not the maker."

This rationale pays off in many ways. Customer requirements were given to our suppliers so that they understood why engineering specifications were changed. This saved time, because the focus was placed on important issues rather than why the changes were made.

Even more benefits are being found as we apply QFD to other programs. Ray Peck of Body and Chassis Engineering is working on a power-steering pump for a 1991 model. He said that QFD is working in ways he never expected. He's excited about how QFD turned developing a power-steering pump into a real team effort. Everyone on the QFD team learned the needs and operations of the other team members. Analytical engineers found out how production engineers applied their concepts. Product engineers and manufacturing engineers began to understand one another better. The machine and tool engineers for Ford and its suppliers were invited to join the team. With a better understanding of all the areas of focus, a more optimum solution was possible. And for the first time, the solution was focused on real customer likes and dislikes.

The end result was a team effort to do things much better and a real learning experience for all the team members. They have new insight on issues they'd never considered before, have a better focus on the overall product, and are much better-prepared to provide a more optimum solution, not only in quality as perceived by the customer, but also in capital investment, size, and all other aspects of the product.

Another very positive advantage of the QFD process is that it provides a way to capture the experience of our experts. It's a common occurrence for an expert to be promoted, get sick, retire, or whatever, and the remaining people don't really have the experience you'd like to have applied to the product. How do you train them? Where is the videotape of your expert's experience? The truth is, it doesn't exist, and you really take a large step backward. But if you've done a formal QFD and kept it up-to-date as new experience and information were acquired, you've captured all that knowledge for younger people to use and to build on. So an intricate part of the QFD process is the recording process. This captures *everything* that's done so it can be applied to the next project for even better results.

I've covered just a few benefits our people using QFD have found. And remember, we're just starting to use the process. We've yet to experience the full benefits that Don Clausing mentioned earlier. But there's no question in my mind that Don is quite right that QFD will help reduce product-development cycles, reduce costs, improve quality, and meet customer needs. Now, don't get me wrong; QFD isn't a panacea. It's a potentially powerful tool, but it's only a tool. And like all tools, it must be used properly to be effective.

Ray Peck told me that his team became so enthralled with the team interaction and learning that take place in the QFD process that their original one-hour meetings quickly expanded to half-day sessions. Fortunately, they didn't lose sight of their mission, and they wisely pulled back and put parameters on how QFD should be used. QFD must be used selectively. It requires such a significant commitment of time and effort that it can't be done on a large scale or with many tasks at one time.

I'd like to briefly share some of the suggestions made by QFD teams at Ford. QFD is the blueprint for quality planning. By quality planning, I mean bringing together the sum of all products, facilities, people, suppliers, and elements needed to get a job done right. When you bring it all together, QFD becomes a management tool for total quality excellence.

When a significant feature or product is being developed, QFD is critical. This is when all the benefits I mentioned earlier really have an impact. Using QFD at that time can give you a real "leg up" in matching customer needs and wants while preventing defects. At the same time, it will help optimize cost, time, weight, and so forth.

But to do all of that requires that we also, within the framework of QFD, use the other disciplines we've learned, such as Finite-Element Analysis, Failure-Mode-and-Effect Analysis, Taguchi Methods, and Design for Assembly. They all have their place within the QFD framework.

QFD should be considered for anything that has a direct bearing on customer acceptance. That's especially true when a product of particular importance to the customer is being developed and when customers have expressed concern about an existing product.

This may seem to cover a broad spectrum, but once

you get involved with QFD, the concepts become clearer. Then you can draw your own parameters as to where it will work best for you.

As I mentioned earlier, we're still implementing QFD at Ford. We don't have all the answers, because we still have a lot to learn. There's one thing for certain, however: We're making a commitment to the process. More than 500 people at Ford have received training in QFD. This training has ranged from one- to three-day workshops. We're working with the American Supplier Institute, Inc., to structure more training programs with a heavy emphasis on workshops so our people can really get a feel for QFD. And we're developing software to streamline QFD planning for even greater efficiency. So you can see that QFD is going to be part of the future at Ford, which means that QFD will be part of the future for our suppliers.

In the years to come, we expect our suppliers to become increasingly involved with our designers, engineers, manufacturing areas, and even other suppliers. We're going to ask our suppliers to learn how we work, and we want them to tell us how they operate. Doing this means more than learning about QFD, it means using it.

The taker isn't just someone who buys a car. In the supplier's case, Ford, General Motors Corp., and Chrysler Corp. are the takers, the customers. Suppliers must meet their customers' needs—which are the same needs Don Clausing described in Chapter 7—better quality, reduced costs, features that appeal to the customer, and shorter development times. This is why no one should brush off QFD. Just as it will help us meet our customers' needs, it can help our suppliers meet *their* customers' needs. If we look at QFD in this light, we can work together as a team.

Teamwork between Ford Motor Co. and its suppliers goes back a long way. Henry Ford I worked with suppliers for five years to develop the components and manufacturing processes for the Model T. During the next 80 years, this teamwork produced a lot of high technology. But that technology hasn't been easy to develop—it still takes us five years to develop a new car.

To be competitive, we must cut that development time in half while improving quality, reducing costs, and being more responsive to customer needs. It can be done: The Japanese have already done it. QFD will help, but it's just a start. We must work together to use QFD as a stepping-stone to go beyond following the competition and to once again become leaders in innovation.

. 10 .

Company-Wide
Quality Control

Lawrence P. Sullivan

It's clear that U.S. companies must change to become more competitive in world markets. The only way we can gain market share is to develop new products in a shorter time frame than the competition and to launch these products with improved quality and lower costs. The question becomes "How can we undertake such a huge task with fewer resources?" Also, "How can we accelerate the rate of improvement so we can increase our competitive position in the years to come?" We've all heard about Japanese strategies, and many have experienced firsthand the methods used by Japanese companies to improve quality and reduce costs.

The point isn't to reiterate success stories from Japan, but to formulate new thinking for U.S. executives that's essential to change the way U.S. companies operate. We'll refer to Japanese Company-Wide Quality

Lawrence P. Sullivan is Chairman of the Board and Chief Executive Officer of the American Supplier Institute, Inc., Dearborn, Michigan.

Control (CWQC) only as a foundation for thinking about how U.S. companies can change.

Japanese-style CWQC, which was initiated in 1968, is significantly different from the traditional Total Quality Control taught and practiced up to this point in the United States. According to Dr. Kaoru Ishikawa, CWQC involves and integrates the activities of all company employees and functions and fosters continuous company-wide education in all elements of quality technology. Integral to CWQC are the President's Audit (e.g., policy management), which deploys company policy through all activities and functions; quality circles; and problem-solving tools and advanced statistical methods. Industrial organizations such as the Japanese Union of Scientists and Engineers, the Japanese Standards Association, and the Central Japan Quality Control Association provide nationwide education and promotion of uniform quality technology. Additionally, the Deming Prize serves as a catalyst for CWQC at many companies.

Japanese Industrial Standard Z8101–1981 provides a uniform national definition of quality control: "A system of means to economically produce goods or services which satisfy customers' requirements. Implementing quality control effectively necessitates the cooperation of all people in the company, involving top management, managers, supervisors, and workers in all areas of corporate activities such as market research, research and development, product planning, design, preparations for production, purchasing, vendor management, manufacturing, inspection, sales and after services, as well as financial control, personnel administration, and training and education. Quality control carried out in this manner is called Company-Wide Quality Control."

In translating this Japanese Industrial Standard to the U.S. way of thinking, CWQC is two things:

- A philosophy that all employees at all levels representing all functions pursue quality in everyday activities. It thus becomes a cultural pattern resulting from top-management leadership and deployment through education and training.
- A horizontal mechanism called Quality Function Deployment (QFD) that facilitates technical interaction between and among all activities and prioritizes the application of quality technology.

CWQC can be viewed as the seven stages of the "Buildup of Quality" shown in **Figure 10-1**. Several major U.S. companies have used this as the pro forma method for adopting CWQC. While all stages are important, the last four (education, parameter design, the Quality Loss Function [QLF], and QFD) will contribute the most toward helping U.S. companies become more competitive. Individual companies, however, should develop internal strategies to achieve the proper blend of all seven stages.

Recently, Dr. Ishikawa provided the following definition of quality, which is very similar to the definition found at most U.S. companies: "To practice quality control is to develop, design, produce, and supply a quality product and service which is most economical, most useful, and always satisfactory to the consumer." Japan and the U.S. define quality quite similarly. A significant difference exists, however, in the implementation and application of quality technology. Understanding what to change will help U.S. companies achieve better results.

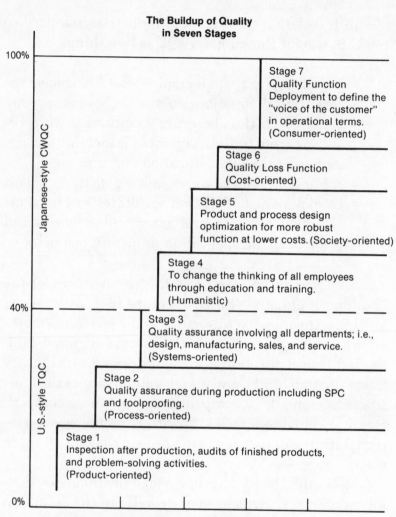

Figure 10–1. Several U.S. companies have used the seven-stage "Buildup of Quality" as the pro forma method for adopting Company-Wide Quality Control.

What to Change

U.S. companies are very successful at creating technology, developing capital resources, and implementing operating systems. Also, U.S. executives are generally intelligent, creative, and decisive, as well as being highly motivated. The solution isn't to scrap everything and start over or to copy Japanese companies. Rather, we must change while simultaneously providing continuity in order to maximize our past achievements. What do we change and how do we achieve the optimum balance between change and continuity? The following six changes must occur in U.S. companies in order to improve the competitive position of U.S. products.

Change #1: We must focus all activities on the voice of the customer rather than the voice of the expert, the engineer, or the executive. This idea first came to light in May 1983 when Dr. Ishikawa visited Ford Motor Co. at the invitation of W. E. Scollard to conduct a series of top-management seminars on CWQC. Over dinner one evening, Dr. Ishikawa expressed his fear that Ford and other U.S. companies concentrate too much on vertical, versus horizontal, quality deployment. He likened this to the weaving of cloth, where the horizontal weave reinforces the vertical weave. At Ford, however, he suggested that the horizontal weave must be stronger than the vertical weave in order to neutralize the voice of the executive and facilitate deployment of the voice of the customer. **Figure 10-2** illustrates this concept. U.S. companies must change from internally oriented quality (specifications and experts) to externally oriented quality (the voice of the customer).

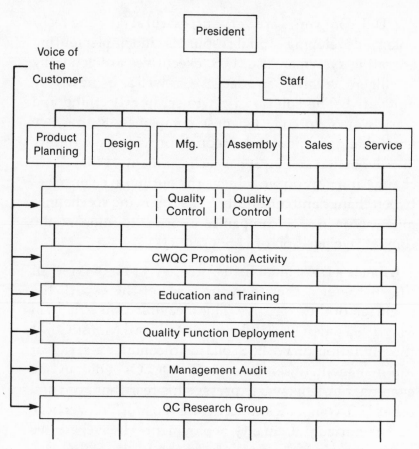

Figure 10–2. In order to neutralize the voice of the executive and facilitate deployment of the voice of the customer, the horizontal weave must be stronger than the vertical weave.

Change #2: We must change the way we think about quality. Quality in the U.S. is traditionally equated with conformance to engineering specifications, and quality improvement is associated with problem-solving activities. Every product, however, has a "best value" for function, fit, and appearance. This best value represents the voice of the customer, which is often different from the voice of the engineer (see **Figure 10-3**). We must promote "target-value quality" in all functions.

Change #3: We must adopt the horizontal mechanism for CWQC and QFD to help integrate and prioritize the application of quality technology in all functions, forming the strong horizontal weave Dr. Ishikawa described.

Change #4: We must apply quality technology to reduce variation in product function and in manufacturing/assembly processing. Traditionally, we try to identify the cause for variability and apply controls to limit or restrict the impact on product function. An entirely new

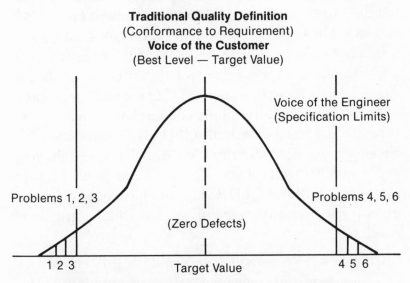

Figure 10-3. Every product has a "best value" for function, fit, and appearance. This best, or target, value reflects the voice of the customer, which is often different from the voice of the engineer.

way of thinking is advanced by Dr. Genichi Taguchi, who has developed Quality Engineering technology to achieve robust function of products and processes, reducing sensitivity to variation and costs.

Change #5: We must view quality technology from the standpoint of priority and how different methods interrelate and learn how each method can be *best* used to support and reinforce our primary objective (improving quality and reducing cost). The mix of quality technology from company to company may be completely different based on their inherent strengths and weaknesses.

On a recent study mission to Japan, we asked Toyota Auto Body Co., Ltd., how quality technology contributed to its dramatic quality improvement from 1977 to 1985. The answer is shown in **Figure 10-4**. Note that Taguchi Methods contributed 50% of the improvement and Statistical Process Control (SPC) 0%. This is because Toyota Auto Body uses SPC to monitor, maintain, and uplift quality (after improvement has been achieved through parameter design). QFD also contributed 0% because it's used to identify the critical items on which to apply quality technology. Toyota Auto Body further stated that without QFD it wouldn't have been effective in applying quality technology to achieve the best results.

Change #6: We must educate and train all employees to understand and apply new quality technology. This is probably the most difficult, and initially most costly, change we face. Ford Motor Co. initiated supplier training under the direction of Dr. W. Edwards Deming in May 1981. This was followed by Taguchi Methods train-

Quality Improvement
1977-85

Quality Method	% Contribution	
	Toyota Auto Body	Others
● Parameter Design (Taguchi Methods)	50	30-70
● Fault-Tree Analysis and		
Reverse Fault-Tree Analysis	35	20-50
● Failure-Mode and Effect Analysis	15	5-20
● Statistical Process Control		
(monitor, maintain, and uplift)	0	0-10
● Quality Function Deployment		
(determine critical items)	0	0

Figure 10-4. A number of quality methods contributed to quality improvement at Toyota Auto Body Co., Ltd., from 1977 to 1985. SPC and QFD are rated at 0% because the former is used to monitor, maintain, and uplift quality; the latter, to identify the critical items on which to apply quality technology.

ing in March 1983 and QFD training in June 1986. Today, Ford has a very inclusive education and training program that involves all levels and all activities. The program includes 48 different courses and requires the application of quality technology on actual product- and process-improvement projects (case studies). The most effective education and training is accomplished through 80% application and 20% lecture.

The Ford program will serve as a model for other U.S. companies to follow. Many companies already have internal training programs in traditional methods. The challenge lies in developing additional education in new quality technology (e.g., QFD and Taguchi Methods) that augments and complements these programs. Companies should develop their own curriculum, resources, and structure to facilitate and carry out their specific management policies.

Summary for Top Management

The responsibility of top management is to organize and direct activities that result in products and services that meet customer requirements (i.e., the voice of the customer). Top management must facilitate quality improvement and cost reduction through the integrated efforts of all employees, associates, and dealers. This is best achieved through company-wide education and training to deploy policy and improve employee technical and operating skills. By achieving uniform levels of knowledge, employees are better able to communicate horizontally and interact on technical issues. The President's Audit (policy management) must be carried out at all levels to embed these ideas in the workplace and to evaluate the results. **Figure 10-5** illustrates the voice of the customer in relation to CWQC through education and training.

Top management's primary task is to improve the personal capability of all individuals within the company, as **Figure 10-6** illustrates. U.S. executives have primarily focused on improving quality by solving problems. If top management concentrates on improving employee capability and the management system, subsequent improvements in products and processes will occur automatically. The Mazda Creed illustrates this point:

"In order to make Mazda synonymous with high

Education and Training

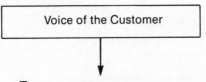

1. High-quality product
2. Low-cost product
3. Robust function — insensitive to:
   A. Variations in environment (climate)
   B. Deterioration in use (wear)
   C. Piece-to-piece variability (production)
4. Attractive-looking
5. Comfortable to use
6. Safe under all conditions
7. Modern features

→ Company-Wide Quality Control

1. Education and training in quality technology
2. Policy deployment by top management
3. Technical interaction through QFD
   A. Market research activities
   B. Product development
   C. Engineering
   D. Manufacturing and assembly
   E. Service activities

→ All Employees — All Functions

Figure 10–5. The voice of the customer is deployed through education and training in Company-Wide Quality Control, which includes application of Quality Function Deployment.

quality and give it a superior image, everyone will participate to improve five qualities: 1) quality of management, 2) quality of work, 3) quality of human behavior, 4) quality of work environment, and 5) quality of product and service."

Note that the number-one priority at Mazda Motor

Management's Role

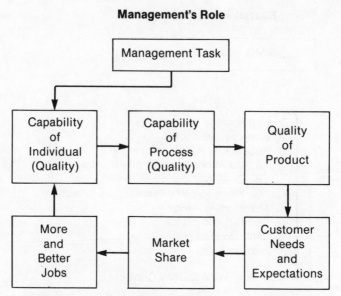

Figure 10–6. Top management's primary task is to improve the personal capability of all individuals within the company.

Corp. is to improve the quality of management, which includes the capability of individuals as well as the management system. The last priority is the quality of product and service. The president of Mazda clearly understands his primary task, the result of which will improve quality, reduce costs, and increase market share.

Prescription for Change

The following "Prescription for Change" is guaranteed to improve market share if—and only if—it's facilitated by top management.

1. Top management should understand the six

changes previously described and foster them throughout the company.

2. The President's Audit (policy management) should be used to carry these ideas into every workplace and evaluate results.

3. A CWQC promotion activity reporting to a top executive (i.e., president or vice president) should be established.

4. QFD should be incorporated as the operating mechanism for CWQC. Leadership should be provided by the chief engineer and results measured by the CWQC promotion activity.

5. Management should develop company-wide education and training based on local needs, technical requirements, and individual capabilities. Quality technologies should be directly related to the "Buildup of Quality's" seven stages.

6. Education and training should include case studies showing simultaneous quality improvement and cost reduction.

7. Case studies should be presented in a management forum within the company for review and comment by top-level engineers.

8. An annual plan for each employee should be established with mutual agreement to improve and evaluate individual capabilities based on achieved results.

9. Top management should evaluate progress through an assessment of reduced engineering changes during product development, time cycles for new product development, and costs (using the QLF); improved quality (through parameter design) and process capability; and in-

creased corporate profit and market share in all product segments.

Knowledge is the only instrument of production that's not subject to diminishing returns. The power to change lies in top management's ability to deploy policy and improve knowledge through all activities and employees.